JOHN COWPER POWYS : LETTERS

Painting in the National Museum of Wales

JOHN COWPER POWYS
A painting by Gertrude M. Powys

JOHN COWPER POWYS
LETTERS 1937–54

Edited

with Introduction and Notes

by

IORWERTH C. PEATE

CARDIFF
UNIVERSITY OF WALES PRESS
1974

*First published in 1974 in a limited edition
by the University of Wales Press
Printed in Wales by Qualitex Printing Limited Cardiff*

© *Iorwerth C. Peate*, 1974
ISBN o 7083 0551

*The University of Wales Press acknowledges, with gratitude,
the financial support given by the
Welsh Arts Council towards the publication of this book*

CONTENTS

	page
Preface	iii
Introduction	v
The Letters	1

ILLUSTRATIONS

Portrait of John Cowper Powys	*Frontispiece*
Facsimile of Letter 37	*after page* 58

PREFACE

THIS volume is offered as a contribution to the steadily-growing literature about John Cowper Powys, to emphasize his deep interest in the language and culture of Wales and his knowledge of them.

I am indebted to the authorities of the National Museum of Wales for permission to print the coloured reproduction of the portrait by Gertrude M. Powys, and to Dr. R. Brinley Jones for his expert guidance in the production of this book.

I. C. P.

November 1973

INTRODUCTION

This book is not an attempt at any kind of literary criticism; but at the outset I must declare my interest in the work of John Cowper Powys. I was attracted to him by the philosophy underlying all his writings, his concept of Time and the necessity of the Imagination:

> There is more on the earth than clay,
> There is more in Time than years.

This is so much in accord with the preoccupation with the concept of Time of the present writer, whose verse is almost completely devoted to its mysteries and who has – on a more mundane level – even tried to assuage the effect of its mesmeric hold upon him by writing of clocks and clockmakers!

In the concluding paragraphs of his *Autobiography*, Powys describes

> the two great electric currents of my life . . . first the gradual discovering and the gradual strengthening of my inmost identity, till it can flow like water and petrify like a stone, and the second the magic trick of losing myself in the continuity of the human generations. By this continuity I mean the way in which from father to son our life-sensations are handed down from the past, creating a sort of 'eternal recurrence' of the poetic mystery of the *little-great* ritual, the daily acts by which we all must live.

In fact, the silver cord of Time.

To me, as a student of folk life, another attraction was his belief in popular culture and his devoted interest in the wide field of material culture, which I nourished by sending him books and papers on the subject. Writing in 1930 of his beloved Walter Pater, he notes that

> No one is more of an adept than he in indicating the manner in which the various inanimate objects which touch the sensibility of exceptional minds affects the symbols of their thought. External objects of all kinds, landscapes, houses, gardens, furniture, the fabrics of dress, the qualities of food and drink, hot and cold airs, the stuff of the soil, the feeling of masonry, the way the light falls, the way the darkness flows – all these things, as he introduces them in his slow, careful reticent, economic

INTRODUCTION

way, yield up their recondite essences and grow little by little to be incorporated and embodied in the shapes and contours of the particular thought for which he is seeking the precise formula.[1]

Powys emphasizes his own same feeling in his *Autobiography*[2]:

Grassy slopes, park-like reaches, winding rivers, pastoral valleys, old walls, old water-mills, old farmsteads, old bridges, old burying grounds, give to the contemplative imagination that poetic sense of *human continuity*, of the generations following each other in slow religious succession, which is what the mind pines for, if it is to feel the full sense of its mortal inheritance.

In his letters here printed, nothing aroused his fury as much as a critic's assertion that our culture was wholly aristocratic in origin and that it was now in ruins. His answer to the Spenglerians is to be found in his 'Pair Dadeni'[3] and in the concluding chapter of his *Autobiography*[4]:

Suppose machinery *does* extend its sway, suppose science in the hands of minority-dictators *does* more and more dominate us, suppose the great battle of the future, with its own particular 'good and evil', comes to be the struggle of the individual to be himself against the struggle of society to prevent him being himself, what we shall have to do will only be what the saints, lovers, artists, mystics have always done, namely *sink into ourselves and into Nature* and find our pleasure in the most simple, stripped, austere and meagre sensations . . . Independence! Independence! That is the secret of all philosophy.

* * * * *

The reason for the publication of these letters is my feeling that Powys's identification with Wales and his own Welshness have been generally ignored. Louis Marlow chose *Welsh Ambassadors* as the title of his 'Powys Lives and Letters'[5] but he quotes Littleton, John Cowper's brother, as saying 'that the family had been in England for four hundred years and that, in spite of its name, there was no real proof of Welsh origin'. Another brother, Albert Reginald (see Letter 18) 'protested that it was "a silly title". He resented it as

---

[1] *The Meaning of Culture*, pp. 41–2.
[2] p. 617.
[3] *Obstinate Cymric* (Carmarthen, 1947), pp. 85–112.
[4] pp. 623–4.
[5] *Welsh Ambassadors* (London, 1936), pp. 47 ff.

INTRODUCTION

pretending and false'. But Louis Marlow held to his title because 'although Powys derivations may be more Saxon than Celtic, every member of this family is, actually, more Celtic than Saxon: in mind, in emotions, and in appearance' and 'because I have no Celtic blood, because I am Saxon and Latin, and entirely Gentile,[6] that . . . I feel . . . John Cowper the most Celtic and Jewish of his family.'

John Cowper himself has described how[7] his 'father's eyes used to burn with a fire that was at once secretive and blazing' when he spoke of how the family was descended from the ancient Welsh Princes of Powys:

> From an old Welsh family long ago established in the town of Ludlow in Shropshire in what were formerly called the Welsh 'Marches' we undoubtedly did – Princes or no Princes – as the genealogies put it, 'deduce our lineage', and I am inclined to think that there has seldom been a mortal soul – certainly no modern one – more obstinately Cymric than my own.

However tenuous his Welsh ancestry may have been, he was intensely aware of it, as his *Autobiography* and his essays on 'Welsh Aboriginals', 'Welsh Culture' and 'Wales and America' in his book *Obstinate Cymric* show. When he was thirty years of age, he bought

> Welsh grammars, Welsh dictionaries, Welsh modern poetry . . ., an elaborate Welsh Genealogy, called 'Powys-Fadoc',[8] and mightily chagrined was I when I found no mention of my father's ancestors in it! I bought everything I could lay hands on that had to do with Wales and with the Welsh people . . . I resolved to realize with my whole spiritual force what it meant to be descended – to the devil with 'Powys-Fadoc', from those ancient Druidic chieftains.[9]

Even then he wondered whether he could sell his house at Burpham in Sussex 'and wander off with my family and my folios to some remote hiding-place in mid-Wales'. At that time he gave up trying to learn Welsh since 'Providence had deprived me of the least tincture of philology'. But even then

---

[6] The Powyses had a maternal great-grandmother who may have been Jewish.
[7] *Autobiography*, p. 26.
[8] J. Y. W. Lloyd, *History of the princes, the lords-marcher and the ancient nobility of Powys Fadog*. 6 vols. (London, 1881–7.)
[9] *Autobiography*, pp. 334–5.

INTRODUCTION

he had misgivings that he was doing wrong 'to the romantic basis' of his nature. Indeed, he felt that if he had followed this 'craving', perhaps he would have managed to learn Welsh. What is not generally known is that after settling in Merioneth he acquired an excellent reading knowledge of the language, although he was shy of writing and of speaking Welsh. Letter 2 is an example of an early attempt in his study of the language to write it.

Jeremy Hooker[10] writes: 'Obviously, in Powys's feeling for "the romance of race" Wales occupies a very special position as the source of his idea of the imagination.' This is true, although Powys's use of the term 'race' is to be deplored: there is no 'Welsh *race*' or an 'English *race*'. But Powys was not concerned with scientific accuracy. 'We Aboriginal Welsh People' he wrote,[11] 'are the proudest people in the world. We are also the humblest . . . Both qualities are peculiar to us as a race and have been so for at least ten thousand years.' This is obvious hyperbole, for only early in the Christian era did the Welsh language develop from the Brythonic, and none of us can pontificate about Welsh characteristics in 8000 B.C.! But to him this belief was of basic importance. So was the Welsh language:

> Deep, unfathomably deep is the instinct that makes us Aboriginals of Wales clinging through thick and thin to a language whose *syntax* and whose *syntax only* is the Merlin-like 'esplumeoir' of our soul. Deep is the instinct that makes us cling through thick and thin . . . to those favoured and privileged ones among us who, inevitably, constantly and naturally *speak our language* and have to *transfer their thoughts* before uttering them in any other. The goal of our aim, the *ael** – if I may be permitted to use a word that the dictionary gives as confined to the Province of Powys – of our intentions, is to increase the number of those who speak and read and write in this language of ours, this language which is the living, growing, forward-looking symbol of the most conqueror-absorbing powers ever possessed by any nation.[12]

---

[10] B. Humfrey (ed.), *Essays on John Cowper Powys* (Cardiff, 1972), p. 54.
[11] *Obstinate Cymric*, p. 7.
* Spurrell (Anwyl)'s dictionary gives *ael* (= 'goal') as confined to Powys, but the University of Wales Dictionary gives its first literary use as 1897.
[12] ibid., pp. 11–12.

INTRODUCTION

Powys, whatever his extravagant claims for the pre-Celtic 'aboriginal Welsh', identified himself completely with those of us who maintain that the preservation and development of the Welsh language are imperative if the Welsh nation is to survive, and of that he had no doubt.

John Cowper Powys did not come to live in Wales because of his 'mania for solitude and independence', or (as Jeremy Hooker seems to imply[13]) in 'rejection of the modern world'. Corwen and Wales, too, are very much part of 'the modern world': it was, as Powys himself states[14] explicitly 'as the fulfilment of an early and youthful longing . . . to return to the land of my remote ancestors'. He came to Corwen in the 1930s, and in his 'Wales and America' gives a vivid and sympathetic description of the Vale of Edeirnion:

> From this little new house which, like the rest is beautifully designed, I can not only look down upon the wide pastoral meadows where as Milton says in Lycidas, 'Deva spreads her wizard stream', but I can look across to the summit of a pre-historic hill-city of unknown antiquity, whose fallen walls make a massive stone-coronet in one place about twenty feet thick, where you can clearly see the ruins of ancient chambers built with carefully-trimmed stones.[15]

This was the Mynydd-y-gaer of his *Porius* (see Letter 42).

I first met John Cowper Powys in 1937. My friends, the late John Morgan and Mrs Elena Puw Morgan, with whom I was staying the night at Corwen, pressed me to visit the 'wonderful man' who was living in a council-estate house, Cae Coed, just above the town. So John Morgan and I climbed the hill to see him. My impression of that first meeting is very similar to that of Evelyn Hardy[16] when she saw him, in his ninety-first year, in his house at Blaenau Ffestiniog, to which he had moved from Corwen in 1955 – this time because of his 'mania for solitude' (Letter 48) – 'a thin long-boned hand holding a book – symbol and augury of what was to come.

---

[13] op. cit., p. 56.
[14] *Obstinate Cymric*, p. 55.
[15] ibid., pp. 56–7.
[16] 'John Cowper Powys: a tribute and impression in his 91st year' in *The Aylesford Review*, V, 1962–3, pp. 9–11.

INTRODUCTION

For Mr Powys lay on a sofa beneath the small room's window, clad in a tweed jacket, corduroy trousers and hand-stitched slippers'. It was an unforgettable evening. He and John Morgan were obviously old friends, and the conversation was lively.

In 1942 I was invited by the proprietor and editor of the weekly *Y Cymro* newspaper to become responsible for and to edit its book-review page. This was (at my request) an unpaid leisure activity. The feature was entitled *Cymru Heddiw* (Wales Today) and, except for signed reviews of books, I wrote under the pseudonym *Y Gwerinwr* (The Common Man). I was privileged to receive the co-operation of a distinguished panel of specialists to review books in their particular fields – Professors E. G. Bowen, W. J. Gruffydd, J. R. Jones, the Rev. Herbert Morgan and several others. In my own contributions I dealt with current problems in Welsh literature, and religious and political life, with an occasional article concerning the English and European scenes. It was this weekly page, that John Cowper Powys read regularly, which cemented our friendship, for, from 1942 until 1948, when I gave up the work to devote all my time – leisure- as well as official working-hours – to the creation of the Welsh Folk Museum, Powys wrote fairly regularly to give his own views on the subjects discussed in *Cymru Heddiw*. His comments showed that he had, as a reader, completely mastered the Welsh language. He took a keen interest in many of the subjects discussed, e.g. my comments on the Salazar régime in Portugal, about his brother Llewelyn's work and about modern Welsh poetry.

In writing about verslibrism, I had quoted the query of that eminent scholar the late Professor P. Mansell Jones, who asked[17]: 'Is not verslibrism the mode of a poetry of Discontinuity typifying a civilisation of disruptions and cleavages heading backward, so far as we know, for chaos? . . . The mature poet attains freedom: the novice of today starts free from scratch. No craft of scansion to be learnt before he plunges headlong into the spontaneities of derived eccentricity

---

[17] 'Who wrote the first "Vers Libre"?' in *Wales*, VII, 1947, pp. 382-9 (reprinted from *The Cornhill Magazine*).

and deliquescent formlessness'. With this view of 'poems that are no poems' (Letter 16) Powys agreed thoroughly, and expressed his views in his long Preface to Huw Menai's *The Simple Vision*. So, though we met, alas, very infrequently, we were (Letter 32) 'thinking along the same lines'. 'I find myself' wrote Powys, in 1947 (Letter 33), 'almost invariably in agreement with your viewpoint'. I valued especially his generous comment (Letter 37): 'For you and I ... understand each other curiously well without need of writing'.

Several of Powys's comments about my own work are embarrassingly generous. They show the generosity of a true friend, but I must impress upon the reader the truth of Louis Marlow's assertion that it was 'natural to [J. Cowper Powys] to transform into qualities of genius the qualities of every person he knew well'.[18]

Readers of the letters may well be irritated by the many dashes, the exclamation marks and the convoluted sentences found in them:

> In his letters he evidently writes very rapidly, and he writes as he talks. Being unable to transfer actual looks or gestures to the paper, he apostrophizes and italicizes instead, and he italicizes with various strokes, as though attempting to define the different kinds of gesture that he would be making if he were in the correspondent's presence. It is because he has from early life been a public speaker that he writes letters, and not only letters, as he does: and that he italicizes and exclaims with this freedom.[19]

Indeed, Powys refers in more than one letter to his 'serpentine manner' of writing. 'I am ... a lecturer, a story-teller, preacher & speaker (even an orator!) *first, & a writer secondly* & therefore *not being an artist* I don't worry over punctuation or even syntax' (Letter 37). Another of his habits in letter-writing was to fill every possible margin on every page.

Forty-eight of his letters are printed here: for various reasons, several others have been excluded. The letters appear in chronological order, and explanatory notes (where necessary) follow each letter.

---

[18] *Welsh Ambassadors*, p. 44.
[19] ibid., pp. 53-4.

THE LETTERS

I

7 Cae Coed Corwen / Merioneth
Oct 13 1937

Dear Mr Iorwerth Peate

I did enjoy getting your letter & I am not *over* worried by finding that the Mabinogion is still our best authority on costumes for I shall be spared further research & moreover (following our only authority in this!) shall be free to use my imagination to the limit!

May I be carried off in a clap of thunder & a fall of mist "dwryf a chawat o nywl" if [I] don't bring in some of this same "pali" to engaging effect.

But I think you & I wouldn't have left out that wonderful glaucous enamel for which Manawydan was indebted to the great master of *Calch Llassar* namely *Lassar Llaes Gynwyt*! and which if he put it on his shoes as well as on his saddles would have been wondrous to look upon.

Thank you so much too for giving me the vol of Y Cymmrodor in w^h Iolo Goch's poem comes. Yes by Heaven I think your hint for a *future* romance is splendid. But meanwhile I must work hard at Owain.

Yrs gratefully

John C. Powys.

This letter followed my reply to a query from J.C.P., who was then working on *Owen Glendower*, concerning early medieval Welsh costume. Unfortunately, nothing had been written on the subject. The second and third paragraphs refer to the story of 'Manawydan son of Llŷr' (see Gwyn Jones and Thomas Jones, *The Mabinogion* (Everyman's Library, 1949).

Dwryf a chawat o nywl = thunder and a fall of mist: *pali* = silk, silk brocade. The University of Wales, *A Dictionary of the Welsh Language*, gives *calch llasar* as 'blue azure, blue enamel', but the late Sir Ifor Williams (*Pedir Keinc y Mabinogi* (Cardiff, 1930), pp. 233–4) tends to favour 'blue-azure *colour*'. Llasar Llaes Gygnwyt (or Gygwyd) came from Ireland.

The reference to 'a future romance' was, if I recall rightly, in answer to my hint that he should write about the Dark Ages in Wales. *Porius* may have been the result.

2

7 Cae Coed / Corwen / Merioneth / N. Wales
Nov 22 1938

Anwyl Mr Iorwerth Peate

Maddeuwch, os gwellwch yn dda, llythyr hwn mor llawn o cymaint o camgymeriadau gyda holl y dreigliadau yng nghyfeiliornus! Ond y mae eisiau genyf dangos i chwi fy ymdrech dysgu yr iaith Brythoneg. Yr wyf wedi darllen – gyda Gciriadur Saesneg a Chymraeg – y Cofiant O. M. Edwards gan Prof W. J. G. a wedi cael ef diddorol iawn ac yn symbylu. Yr wyf yn ddymuno ei bod yn ysgrifennu yr ail rhan! Yr wyf wedi ddarllen hefyd y llyfr rhyfeddol "Bywyd a Gwaith Moses Williams" gan John Davies; er yn fynych yr oedd rheidiol imi chwilio allan pob gair unigol brawddeg!

Yr wyf eisioes wedi cyrraedd y dudalen 900 – dyma osgoiasaf yr iaith Gymraeg! – yn fy rhamant am Owain Glyndwr – mewn fy llawysgrifen, yr wyf yn rhoi i chwi ar ddeall, y rhai yn fawr iawn ydyw, fel yr wyt yn weled!

Ond i fy neges! Byddaf yn dref o Penybont ar Ogwr yn Sir Forgannwg (Bridgend in Glamorganshire) Rhagfyr pumed (Dec 5th) rhoi darlith am "Pedeir Keinc y Mabinogi" gan wneud defnydd o Prof J. W. G.'s "Math" ac Dr Ifor Williams – hwy ill deuoedd; ond gan geisio rhoi arno fy nehongliad hefyd – yn rhoi imi yddynt y gyflog o "Ten Guineas". Y mae arnaf ofn mai yr wyf yn dweud rhy diweddar, ond ai buasai ef yn ddichonadwy i chwi trefnu darlith am un testun ac at yr un gyflog yng Nghaerdydd ac ar dydd nesaf sef – Dydd Mawrth (Dec 6th) Rhagfyr chweched? Bydd ef, wrth gwrs, yn weddus iawn imi os buasaf mynd i Gaerdydd a rhoi fy ddarlith dacw, dydd Mawrth *Rhagfyr chweched*: ond gan adnabod y fyr amser y mae arnaf ofn mai dyddiad hwn yn annichonadwy ydyw. Ond, os gwellwch yn dda cynnullwch mewn eich meddwl fy bod i bob amser yn barod myned i Gaerdydd o wrth y fan hon – oddi wrth Corwen (ach y fi! Nis gwn pa un bynnag "oddi wrth" y mae yn dreiglio y "C" yng Nghorwen!). Deg o giniau hon yng nghynnwysol (inclusive) ydyw; ac, wrth gwrs, talaf fy daith a fy llety. Ym Mhridgend (dyma treigliad yn dda!) – a fy glust fedr cael y rheswm *yna*! – yddynt yn rhoi imi (nis gwn amser berf yn nyfodol) lletygarwch; ond rhaid i mi beidio disgwyl hwn pob man, fel pregethwr hen – ond eu derbyniadau, yr wyf ofn arnaf, mwy apostolaidd oeddynt! Y mae fy nyledswydd i dweud i chwi mai yr wyf darlithiwr hen heb ddannedd ond fel rhyfelfarch hen o'r llwyfan, y ddannedd yng ngholl y mae yn wneud gwahaniaeth bychan!

Yr wyf yn gael "*Y Brython*" bob Dydd Iau a wyf yn mwynhau eich llythyrau ynddo. Dymunaf eich fod yn ysgrifennu ateb wrth *Owain Tudur* yn amddiffyn o nofelydd diweddar erbyn y gormes delfrydyddol o *Plato* ac ei gwerinlywodraeth yn ffasgaid!

Y mae gennyf hiraeth dangos pa beth y chwedloniaeth Cymraig yn wahanol ydyw a rhagorach iawn rhag y Gwyddelig; ond och! oll o fy awdurdodau dangosant eu tebygrwydd, nid y gwahanol rhwngynt.

Maddeuwch cwbl camgymeriadau. Eiddoch yn wir

John Cowper Powys.

Translation of Letter 2

Dear Mr Iorwerth Peate

Please forgive this letter so full of so many mistakes and all its mutations wrong! But I want to show you my effort to learn the Brythonic language. I have read – with an English-Welsh dictionary – Prof W. J. G[ruffydd]'s biography of [Sir] O[wen] M. Edwards and found it very interesting and stimulating. I wish he would write the second part! I have also read the wonderful book "The Life and Work of Moses Williams" by John Davies; although frequently I had to search for every word in a single sentence!

I have already reached page 900 – here I can avoid the Welsh language! – in my romance about Owain Glendower in my own handwriting, you must understand, which is very large as thou seest!

But to my message! I shall be in the town of Bridgend in Glamorganshire on Dec 5th to give a lecture on "The Four Branches of the Mabinogi" making use of Prof J. W. [= W. J.] G[ruffydd]'s "Math" and of Dr Ifor Williams – both of them; but attempting to give my own interpretation too. They are giving me the sum of Ten Guineas. Though I fear that I am too late in mentioning it, would it be possible for you to arrange a lecture on the same subject and at the same price in Cardiff on the next day, that is Tuesday Dec 6th? It would suit me well, of course, if I went to Cardiff and gave my lecture there on Tuesday, December the sixth: but knowing how short is the notice, I fear that this date may be impossible. But please keep in mind that I shall always be prepared to go to Cardiff from this place – from Corwen (ugh! I do not know whether *oddi wrth* mutates the "C" in Corwen!) It would be ten guineas inclusive: and, of course, I pay my own travelling and lodging. At Bridgend (that's a good mutation!) – and my ear gets the reason *there*! – they give me (I don't know the future tense) hospitality: but I must not expect this everywhere, like the old preacher[s] – but their receipts, I fear, were more apostolic! It is my duty to tell you that I am an old lecturer without teeth, but as an old war-horse of the platform, the lost teeth make a slight difference!

I get the *Brython* [newspaper] every Thursday and enjoy your letters in it. I wish you would write to answer *Owain Tudur* defending a recent novelist against Plato's idealistic oppression and his fascist republic!

I long to show how different and superior is Welsh mythology as contrasted with the Irish; but alas all my authorities stress their similarity and not their differences.

Forgive all the mistakes. Yours truly

John Cowper Powys.

The original of this letter is now in the National Library of Wales (N.L.W. 2340C). In it, J.C.P.'s Welsh is very faulty, especially his mutations. But it was a brave attempt by one who assured me many times that he had 'no ear' for languages. He came to *read* Welsh well, but would not attempt to write it.

3

7 Cae Coed / Corwen / Merioneth / N. Wales
March 3 1942

Dear Dr Peate

I can't tell you how proud & pleased your most welcome letter made me. The pleasure you gave me was well worth the effort of putting your generous impulse into words. It w^d. be of the deepest interest & value to me if one of these days when the calls upon your time lessen a bit – for I can believe at this moment after your victory over your enemies on which nobody could congratulate you more sincerely than I do, you are needing and drawing upon all your energy to consolidate both your psychic & practical position – I say if one of these days you *did* really launch out, freely & frankly, on the subject of my "Owen"; appreciating where you *do* appreciate & criticizing where you feel I've wandered from the right track . . . Yours is the one letter I've had from any of the Welsh-speaking & Welsh-writing intellectual leaders and this renders it peculiarly & especially precious; and indeed what shall I say? an *event* to me. I'm a wretched linguist myself but though (owing you might suppose to having an actual hole in my head where the faculty for catching the *oral music* of words ought to be) I shall I fear (for I am 70 next October) never speak or follow the language spoken – I am getting on, by persistent industry, *very nicely* in reading it – I read the "Baner" (*Y Faner*) *from beginning to end even including* the Maes-y-lafur Dydd Sul Ysgol! every week & the "Llenor" whenever I can get hold of a copy & the "Seren" of Bala of course. And my *secret* ambition w^h. I now whisper in your ear, is one day to be able to join in these exciting *controversies*. Nothing could be more interesting to my *particular kind* of mind than the subtle & *complicated clashings* of the various political, religious & cultural schools of thought in Wales today.

I'm just off to give a talk on "King Lear" to Prof. Gwyn Jones' English Study Club at Aberystwyth & he is going to put me up for a couple of nights. This is a serious undertaking to a demi-semi-invalid like me but I have *never been to Aberystwyth*; so you can imagine how the adventure excites me.

Damn! no margins left – for anything – but my very best regards.

Yrs J. C. Powys.

P.S. If ever you were inspired to write to me *in Welsh* – with your clear hand I am convinced I could follow every word.

In this letter J.C.P. replies to the note which I had sent to him congratulating him on his *Owen Glendower*. The reference to my 'victory' was to events in 1941 when, in August of that year, my declared pacifism (I had been exempted unconditionally from service in the armed forces as a conscientious objector) led to my dismissal from my museum keepership by the then National Museum of Wales Council, and my reinstatement by the Court of Governors of the Museum which – under the leadership of the late Professor W. J. Gruffydd and R. Moelwyn Hughes, K.C. – in October 1941 repudiated the Council's action.

In 1942, Professor Gwyn Jones, now of University College, Cardiff, was Professor of English in the University College of Wales, Aberystwyth.

4

7 Cae Coed / Corwen / Merioneth
March 12 1942

Dear Mr Iorwerth Peate,

I was delighted to get your letter of the 10th.

No! except that Adelphi one by E. Myers (who sent it to me herself!). The English Reviews arent of any interest at all – totally uncritical! – well! the one you speak of & the one in the Observer by Swinnerton I think – but I'm not going to worry about seeing any more! But I *shall* look forward to *any* I can get *hold of* in Welsh – the 1st Welsh one was in "Seren" y Bala by my Llandderfel friend Mr Evan Roberts. This came out a week before Publication Day! And if it is reviewed in "Llenor" I trust I shan't miss it – but for some reason neither the Autumn nor Winter "Llenor", as far as I know, have yet reached our mutual friends the Morgans – (I am glad to say Mr Morgan is home again from the Liverpool Hospital and very slowly but *I trust surely* recovering) and they always have hitherto lent me their copy.

As to the *little harp* I must, my dear Peate, throw up my hands & cry "a hit, a palpable hit!" Of course you are right. It comes over me with your words like a convincing thunderclap. And my lady here says she has read *somewhere* about the little harps played *ar y gliniau* & not as I thought, without due consideration of the subject – *between* the knees. Well my friend it was just pure *simple ignorance* of music and musical instruments. I must have seen old illustrations of Gray's "Bard" or Scott's "Minstrel" representing a big harp or probably in my ignorance of musical instruments I "went by" the big harp – the only kind I've ever seen – and *even* this I've only seen *here* in the Eisteddfodau! But that you are right about the old Bards' harps being the little sort comes to me now as absolutely proved by Homer's description of the blind minstrel at the court of King Alcinous where it says his "harp" was *hung up on a peg over his head*. I take it the Greek word *Phorminx* is *almost* the same as a harp – tho' often translated "lyre" or "cithara" –

but any way *Phormiktes* is translated in Liddell & Scott's Greek Dictionary (Lexicon I should say) as lyre-player or harp-player. Demodicus the blind bard has his Phorminx hung at the banquet ek passalóphi from a peg "hyper kephales" above his head. It had 7 strings the Lexicon says & was portable i.e. carried by a strap over the shoulder.

In Book XXII of the Odyssey where Phemus, the son of Terpes, is begging for his life when Odysseus finds him playing to the sailors he stood with the "clear-toned lyre" "Phorminx ligeia" "in his hands" "en cheiressin" and later he lays the *hollow* phorminx "phorminx glaphurén" "*on the ground*" "chamase" "between the mixing bowl and the silver-studded chair". Now if only I had been told by *any one* that this great lumbering harp of my mental vision *wasn't* the one used in old times I'd have thought of the "hollow lyre" with its 7 strings! But it may be that it is the "*crwth*" yes! the *crwth* & *not* the *telyn* that is like the Greek "lyre" – Pughe's Dictionary says it has 6 strings and that it so closely resembles the violin that the word is often used for *both* instruments. But all this is *Double-Dutch* to me whose ignorance of these matters you'd not credit as possible in a romantic & poetical novelist like myself!

P.S. I'm *very* disappointed to learn that so far this curst lack of paper has hindered the publication of your "Hanes Diwylliant Gwerin Cymru" for 'tis *exactly* what w^d. have interested O so many of your readers – including your latest but not the least interested! I hope in the course of this year to write (in English) one of those *yellow booklets* (that Mr William Griffiths of Foyle's is publishing about this country) *on the Mabinogion*. At the moment I am deep in the exciting & lively and even violent controversy between *Mr Timothy Lewis* whom I met in Aberystwyth and the Rhys – Morris-Jones – Ifor Williams tradition. I suppose you'd hardly care (in this lively & touchy controversy between such formidable paleographists & experts) to sum up for me your own attitude to this important matter. It certainly seems for I've got those two Cymmrodor numbers that Morris-Jones was one too many for Dr Gwenogvryn Evans but Timothy Lewis seems no mean adept with the weapons of scholarly controversy! Don't hurry about replying – for you are more busy than I am; tho' this weakness of *my eyes* makes my work-days all too brief!

Well, I *must* stop – 'Tis, as I say, this whoreson weakness in *my eyes* that led me into the temptation of writing such awful scrawls! Forgive me, my dear Mr Peate!

Yrs to command
John C. Powys.

This was in reply to a letter in which I had drawn J.C.P.'s attention to a review of *Owen Glendower* by Elizabeth Myers in *The Adelphi*, and had suggested that his description of the harp in the novel was incorrect, the large triple harp being no earlier than the end of the seventeenth century. Mr Evan Roberts of Llandderfel, a well-known bibliophile and local historian, was a mutual friend and will appear again in several of the letters. 'The Morgans' were John Morgan and his wife, Mrs Elena Puw Morgan, of Annedd Wen, Corwen. The late John Morgan, a native of Y Foel, Llangadfan, Montgomeryshire, was well-known in Welsh literary circles as a good poet in the strict metres. Mrs Morgan, winner of the National Eisteddfod Prose Medal, was the author of several novels in the Welsh language.

The postscript refers to my book *Diwylliant Gwerin Cymru* (Welsh Folk Culture) published in 1942. Mr Timothy Lewis (uncle of Alun Lewis the poet) was at one time Reader in Palaeography in the University College of Wales, Aberystwyth, and the author of a work on Welsh Medieval Law. A man of much erudition, his critical faculty was strangely warped as was evidenced by the fanciful arguments with which he strove to demolish the scholarship of Sir John Rhŷs, Sir John Morris-Jones, Sir Ifor Williams and others.

ar y gliniau = on the knees.

5

7 Cae Coed / Corwen / Merioneth / N. Wales
March 30 1942

Dear Dr Iorwerth Peate

Most grateful was I for your good letter of the 26th. You've told me just the things I want to know about the harp. Aye! but I like the idea of the early Welsh harp having *hair strings* like the true harp of Apollo "that makes the heaven *drowsy* with this harmony" – tho' that's a funny sort of praise, but the meaning must be to give the gods an ecstasy of the opium-drug sort or "haschish" kind, at least so I take it, with Coleridgean Kubla-Khan visions and "ancestral voices prophesying" – I fear I'm too ignorant of music & musical instruments to know what the word "chromatic" really means in what you tell me Galpin says.

Well! I am so grateful to you, too, for your excellent advice to get a volume of my "Owen" into Prof. Gruffydd's hands. The Publishers have no more available, so I took your suggestion in a still bolder & better way by despatching at once to the address you so kindly gave me at Penarth a copy *inscribed*, with a very brief note (in my best "Pigeon" or "Rook" Welsh) – but in my impetuous haste I committed the "ansyberwyt" of not consoling with the Professor for being in Hospital – but I pray it isn't a serious visit to that ominous place. Yes I know his "Math"; though I haven't got a copy of it now any more, for somebody has stolen the one I had – but I have *not* seen his study of the Mabinogion in the Cymmrodorion of about 1912–1914 *nor* have I seen his article in the Llenor of 1931 (or whenever it was) on Timothy Lewis' books.

I like to think of you having an evening with Gwyn Jones & I trust it materialized O.K. I must look up in Gronwy Owen's letters wh[n]. I've got hwyl – God! what a *scholar he* was! – for a really old-fashioned way of ending up this scrawl! Yes! *here's* a nice one – eich ufudd wasanaethwr o ewyllys da – J. C. Powys.

P.S. I didn't miss, or take lightly, I can assure you, your word of warning over friend T.L.'s excursions. I wanted so much to know what you felt yourself.

Professor William John Gruffydd, M.A., D.Litt., D.-és-L. (1881–1954), was Professor of Celtic in the University College of South Wales, Cardiff, from 1918 to 1946. He was a poet of eminence and one of the two main creators of the Welsh literary renascence of the first half of the twentieth century. He was pre-eminent as a literary critic, and edited *Y Llênor*, a quarterly journal, from 1922 to 1951. Outstanding as a University administrator, he was M.P. for the University of Wales from 1943 until university representation was abolished. A student of Sir John Rhŷs at Oxford, he followed Rhŷs in his studies of Welsh folk-lore, particularly of the Mabinogion; his books, *Math vab Mathonwy* (1928) and *Rhiannon* (1953) are well known. Unrivalled as a prose-writer, his *Hen Atgofion* (1936) and his biography of Sir Owen M. Edwards (1937) are classics of their kind.

Ansyberwyt = discourtesy.

Goronwy Owen (1723–69), cleric and poet, one of the outstanding figures of the Welsh literary tradition.

Eich ufudd wasanaethwr o ewyllys da = Your obedient servant of good will.

6

7 Cae Coed / Corwen / Merionethshire / N. Wales
Nov 6 1943

Dear Doctor Iorwerth Peate

What a wonderful letter for me to get is this from you! In the first place let me praise you from my heart for your noble efforts on behalf of our friend at Llandderfel which do really look from what I can see as if they were destined to be crowned with *success*. And next I do want so much to tell you how thrilled I am by every single word you say about my brother Llewelyn's letters, which are exactly as you describe them for the word graciousness is the happiest possible word for that particular sort of mellow and engaging charm which was so marked a part of his striking personality. Louis Wilkinson has just sent me a Review of this book in the *Sunday Times* of Oct 31 which is really the limit! It begins thus:

"Ll. P. as a letter-writer was made by marriage"
and then it goes on

"the 1st hundred pages reveal a mind utterly and painfully preoccupied with symptoms of illness".

It ends: "The old themes – desire to be published – overwhelming affection for his family – influence of the countryside & private morality that is an odd product for a Somerset Parsonage are transfigured *after his marriage to Miss Gregory* (& how *furious* she will be!) by *a new bright light*"!!! What a mind is revealed in this review eh? It is *extraordinary* how Llewelyn's personality has always *infuriated* the typical journalistic and modern newspaper review mind! It is his *unguardedness* & *childlike innocence* (mixed with shrewd, sly & yet naive mischief!) that excites a curious & quite special hostility that is almost like *a physical desire to beat him up*!

And now let me express to you my dear Dr Peate my personal pride & pleasure at your *most* generous words in regard to that portrait in my sister's lace-shop in New York which really is the only good picture I've ever seen done of myself. Augustus

John began one of my brother *Theodore* in Dorset but alas! he never finished it & I suppose destroyed it. But I will most certainly send your most kind letter to my sister Marian in New York and see what she says!! It *is* a splendid picture by a fine artist called *Raymond Jonson* living I believe now in Santa Fé New Mexico. As to any *other* picture if *this* one is not forthcoming – let us imitate our Politicians, Doctor, & "wait & see" – I confess I feel – but you are a good psychologist and can imagine! – a quaint mixture of *nervous scare & pride. However*! let us wait a bit & see! I am certainly most deeply conscious, my dear Iorwerth Peate, of your own friendliness in this matter & you are especially good to think of your friends – both of your Llandderfel historian and of your historical novelist at a time when you are so pressed & occupied. Yrs most sincerely

John C. Powys.

P.S. I *say*! but what a good article on the *sonnet* you had some weeks ago in *Y Cymro*.

This letter refers to an appeal which we were then organizing, with the help of other friends such as the late Archbishop MacGrath and Rhys J. Davies, M.P., to obtain a Civil List Pension for Evan Roberts of Llandderfel.

The last paragraph refers to a request which I made to J.C.P. that a portrait of him should be included in the Welsh National Portrait Collection in the National Museum of Wales. As will become evident in later letters, his sister Gertrude agreed to paint a portrait of him: this is now in the National Museum (see Frontispiece).

7

7 Cae Coed / Corwen / Merionethshire
Nov 12th 1943

My dear Doctor,

I am simply *thrilled* by your noble words about Llewelyn & your *splendid choice* of a quotation from those letters! I have just seen the anonymous notice or review in *Punch* w^h. again is un-appreciative & un-sympathetic. He certainly must be out of touch with the English reviewers of this particular moment. I have spent all this morning translating your words to send to Miss Gregory who is rendered sad & discouraged by so much hostility & lack of appreciation. But your words will put new heart into her I know. Aye! I wish – as I tell her in my letter – that Llewelyn's Father could have read what you say – he would have agreed *with every single word* (Rev^d. tho' he was!). And he would have been so moved & stirred by the fact that his son's best appreciation & understanding have, from the start, been in the land of *his* fathers. For it is my own experience too just as with Llewelyn – I've never known what it was to be appreciated *after my own heart* for not *all* appreciation tastes good – & sometimes a person prefers to be damned than to be praised in a false & sentimental sort of way. But what you have here done for Llewelyn is wonderful and I thank you from my heart for it; indeed from all of us "as a family" – *chwedl* Evan Roberts!

Oh yes & I was so pleased with that article *giving it to* (in the sound sense of showing him up in his true colours) that villain *Signor Salzazar* whom I've always grudged to see so commended in "Cwrs y Byd" in Y Faner! (By the way, isn't it quaint how "*give it to*" can be used for a good thrashing as I use it here or "give it to him" in the sense of praising him highly. Aye I *did* read your lambasting of Salzazar with pleasure!)

But perhaps you do not write regularly under "Gwerinwr" I hope most heartily you *will* go on writing for it. I can see Y Cymro is much more *popular* tho' in a sense a less "highbrow" paper than Y Faner. Everybody here reads it. You should see the pile of them that arrives by train today! I love to think of your ideas with which I am in such *great* sympathy having such wide publicity. I liked it so well when you countered (long ago!) S[aunders] Lewis's tendency to mediterraneanize Welsh tradition and you emphasized the *Nordic* influence tho' not going *quite* as far, I dare say, as that gallant warrior for *his* "Truth", my admired Mr Timothy Lewis!

Oh yes – and it is a great relief to me, Doctor, that we're (& quite correctly) thinking of my sister Gertrude's picture and not of that youthful one that my sister Marian has in N. York by Raymond Jonson of New Mexico. For this latter word of yours has *just come in time to stop me* writing to Marian (my sister in N.Y.) about *that* picture. For of course I would love above all things for a work of my sister Gertrude to be in the Museum. Only I think she had better do an absolutely new & fresh one! For the one she *did* do of me was done at Montacute long long ago – o I should say fifty years ago – and both Gertrude & I have grown more interesting and individual (at least we've tried to!) than we were in those youthful days. She has promised to come & pay us a visit this ensuing year and she could bring a canvas & her paints! If I went to *her* she'd be so much more interrupted by domestic cares though she never let her painting go and lately she's been painting our friend Louis U. W. (whose appearance "Punch" mocks at Miss Gregory for describing!) but if she came here it w^d. be a holiday for her and she'd be able to take her time – and the longer she was the longer we'd have her company w^h. is always such a delight to Phyllis & me. *She* (Phyllis) by the way has gone to Liverpool today (I don't like the look of the rain) to see her *American cousins* on behalf of herself, her mother & aunt, for we're quite an American colony in Cae Coed as you may know! She'd hoped that Mrs Morgan might have gone with her but this latter lady wasn't I expect given notice in time or she might have gone too; I wish they'd hurry up and bring out "Y *Graith*" but all publishers are the same – I have 2 books: one on "The Art of Growing Old" and one on Dostoievsky in 2 different Publishers' hands but it's a case of *hope deferred* as to their appearance wait, wait, wait "you can't feed capons so".

Yes I would be ever so much happier to have a new picture by Gertrude than that youthful one of Jonson's that Marian has, Besides, Marion is "precious", as we say, "of it" and very likely is thinking of leaving it to her son out there if he ever settles down. And any way she is *lonely* over there & that picture in her lace-shop in Madison Avenue in that great city may have grown to be a companion to her. So I am relieved, my dear Doctor, on all these heads, that you had Gertrude in your mind.

Yrs as ever

John Cowper Powys,
and Phyllis sends her best regards and respects.

This letter was prompted by an appreciation which I wrote in *Y Cymro* (November 13, 1943) of *The Letters of Llewelyn Powys* (John Lane, London).

'*Chwedl* Evan Roberts' = 'as Evan Roberts would say'. *Y Graith* (Aberystwyth, 1943) was a novel by Mrs. Elena Puw Morgan.

8

7 Cae Coed / Corwen / Merionethshire / N. Wales
Nov 20 1943

My dear Iorwerth

I'm thoroughly pleased at your excellent permission *thus* to address you; & I want to thank you very much too for the *Mari Llwyd* [*sic*] paper (in English). Aye! but this is the sort of thing I like best of all, these myths that go deep & *not only* back so far! I think as I read it of a passage in Walter Pater where he speaks of an image somewhere of Demeter the earth-mother depicted with a *Horse's Head*. Yes I certainly *do* possess your "Diwylliant Gwerin Cymru". I ordered it straight from Gwasg y Brython.

As I write this pretty late for me on the evening of the 19th to be posted tomorrow there is actually a *birth taking place* at No. 3 Cae Coed and this – I pray all goes well! – makes me think how the grandmother of the new-born (may it *be* safely dragged through the roof of our *Dimension*!) – brought to us on the eve of all saints' day very early in the morning a present unexpected (most welcome) of *potatoes*. These were deposited on our threshold but the explanations were somewhat obscure save that *it was a custom when she was little* and always "for the eve of All Saints"! Is it the *eve* of all saints that is *"all hallows"*? and is *"all hallows"* the same as *All Souls Day*? I always get mixed up over these dates.

My sister writes that she *did* paint a picture of me in 1929 that is mentioned by Louis Wilkinson (Marlow) – but she says she agrees with me that it would be more exciting & interesting to *paint a new one* & she speaks of "bringing a canvas" here & spending a week with us *early in May* when she will get *"a good light"* in this upstairs room!

A book in Welsh I've not got yet – by Mr Payne to whom you introduced me in your office once – but must get it for

I belong to that Club, is the one praised so well of late by
Y Gwerinwr – by Ll Walters I think.

Yrs as heretofore & I hope to be

J.C.P.

P.S. I do pray we really shall see you soon here your own self in person.

The book referred to in the last paragraph was by my former Museum colleague, Mr Ffransis G. Payne, entitled *Chwaryddion Crwydrol ac Ysgrifau Eraill* (= Strolling Players and other Essays), 1943.

9

7 Cae Coed / Corwen
Dec 29 1943

My dear Iorwerth

Now *you* must leave out the "Mr" too! I should say it *is* a mad piece of silly facetiousness to say that Welsh culture is fundamentally, in its essence, yn ei hanfod, an aristocratic culture. It's the craziest thing I've ever heard. Why, Welsh culture is – But I "carry coals"! But I've *just read* this article of this fellow in Y Faner and I certainly *do* take (and in all seriousness too) "y perl a ganlyn" (as he sarcastically says) which *to me* is a *literally true deep-sea pearl* out of the ultimate oyster under the coiled bulk of the World-Serpent at the bottom of the abysmal ooze!

As a matter of fact, *my* only bother in all this is that in my dictionary, Anwyll Spurrell's, the lexicog refuses to give *any* word beginning "mamal"! All his "mam" compounds run in "o" and "i" like mamol and mamog. No it is *not*, my good Master, *not* evolutionists "wedi rhedeg ar wyllt" and this very catch with which he closes "yr wyf i yn eich caru chwi am i chwi yn gyntaf garu eich epil" *is* absolutely & profoundly *true*.

The thing is this, Iorwerth dear friend, you either possess the *mythological mind or you don't*! And you & I do, & this gentleman doesn't. I expect you are wise to stop at present. But when you *do* at some later time . . . may be in *Y Cymro* . . . refer to this topic, I confess I'd like to see you go after the chap on general metaphysical and philosophical grounds . . . get at him with the Aristotelian entelecheia! Get at him with some quotation from Faust, get after him with the prehistoric *Matriarchy* of these Isles! Let Demeter herself with her Horse's head – "Our Lady of the Stable"! – pursue him over the ploughed field where she lay with *Jasion*! God! he could be attacked in so many different ways – *paradoxically* (er enghraifft) à la Chesterton. He's such an one as is best answered by that chief thing he leaves out, the *atmosphere* of our lives!

But I must get back to Rabelais! Yes, my friend, all Pioneers are abused. We must read Walt Whitman on that topic.

Your faithful admirer & friend
J.C.P.

My Welsh book on Welsh Folk Culture published in 1943 was reviewed in *Y Faner* by Mr Alwyn D. Rees, of University College, Aberystwyth, who maintained that folk culture was aristocratic in origin. I replied critically to this contention. Mr Rees wrote a second time (December 22, 1943) to defend his thesis. John Cowper Powys was much incensed by Mr Rees's statements, but I wrote to tell him that I did not intend to notice further the (somewhat personal) statements made by Mr Rees and inviting J.C.P., if he so wished, to write on the subject in my literary page in *Y Cymro*. Letter 9 was his immediate reaction, to be followed ultimately by his '*Y Pair dadeni* or The Cauldron of Rebirth' which appeared in Welsh in *Y Cymro* (April 13, 1945).

Y perl a ganlyn = 'the pearl which follows'. *Wedi rhedeg ar wyllt* = 'running wild'. *Yr wyf i yn eich caru chwi am i chwi yn gyntaf garu eich epil* = 'I love you because you have first loved your offspring'.

10

7 Cae Coed / Corwen / Merioneth
Jan 5 1944

My dear Iorwerth

Come on! If I can overcome my Berber–Brython–Scotch–English–Swiss–Jewish shyness & call you *Iorwerth* thou canst do as much & call me *John*! J.C.P. is however a very pretty compromise but *Iorwerth* & *John* are both dignified names – 'tisn't as if we proposed like a pair of continental monarchs to call ourselves Nicky & Ticky & Micky or Licky or any other damned comical abbreviation!

I am (and so is Phyllis) so thrilled at your news of a good or better article on Llewelyn in the "Lit. Sup." of the Times and also *extremely relieved* (for very practical and very urgent *economic reasons*!) to hear of an announcement of that old age book. I rejoice to hear of your admiration for Marcus Tullius Cicero. I think very highly of that great old Democratic Orator. 'Tis true he had the vanity of an author but God help us! so have we all! But vanity of *his* sort is entirely pardonable, & *really* entirely *superficial*. Neither for good or ill is it comparable with *Pride*! Not by vanity or ambition, but by *pride* "fell the angels"! Well there it is. But *there are* who are "too proud to fight" i.e. too proud to be vain, conceited *or* ambitious. I try to aim at *this* form of Satanism myself!

But listen! oughtn't I to read the chap's "Adfeilion" "ruins" was it? Have you a copy you could lend me, I swear I'd return it safe? But I know I'm *not* to be trusted about returning books or pamphlets. So tho' I swear, I *warn* you at the same moment & in the same breath. Anyway I mustn't stop to do it at once for it's a matter of *bara and Te* (I won't ever say "ymenyn"!) for me to get this Rabelais book done. But yes I'd dearly love one day – but I *must* finish my Rabelais book first but I hope to do that by All Fools Day – to write an article answering that aristocratic culture-theory of his as applied to "Diwylliant Gwerin Cymru" and with you to translate it for the "Cymro". Heavens! my dear Iorwerth I'd be glad enough any day for my reputation to w^h. you refer is alas! very much – what's that French expression meaning "success of esteem" (I daren't risk the accents!) and not (for I'm no good at standing up to publishers: those unblushing capitalistic employers of *all us writers*) success of income! I would love to write that article defending your position over this culture business for you are one of those Welshmen who do more than *hold an opinion* who *embody* this peculiar & unique human attitude w^h. we call Welsh culture. And I surely will & before Spring is out too! – only I think I ought to glance over the chap's book first – for his attacks on you are not very illuminating as to his *positive* contribution.

Yrs as ever

John.

Bara, *Te* = Bread, Tea. *Ymenyn* = Butter (which he rejected because of his stomach troubles).

II

7 Cae Coed / Corwen / Merionethshire / N. Wales
Jan 11 1944

My dear Iorwerth

It is so very nice of you to be so gracious & reluctant over your old friend's Christian name & heaven forbid I should tease or bully you about it – indeed I *resemble you* in this very peculiarity for I never could bring myself to call Theodore Dreiser *Theodore* & compromised by always calling him Dreiser as indeed he usually signs himself which is a *prouder* way of signing oneself than any other as the Lords of the Privy Council & Bishops sign themselves by their titles so a writer signing himself *simply "Dreiser"* makes the biggest claim; for 'tis one on Posterity & *thoroughly deserved* in his case! In the case however of Edgar Lee Masters with whom I am even perhaps more at ease than with Dreiser I flatly rebelled at calling him *Edgar Lee* though he always calls me "Jack" but I *even to his face* & my Phyllis the same always have called him & obstinately insisted on it at the risk of annoying him, *Mr Masters*. He will be always Mr Masters to us & when we speak of him together in absolute privacy we always call him "Mr Masters" – I dodge the issue in writing to him, in true Welsh fashion beginning "F'annwyl Gyfaill" or "my dear old friend" but the fact remains that in *his* case it also is just (as you say) with me, for I am curst or blest with a regular Boswellian hero-worship for writers I admire and when I say Mr Masters it is as if I said Mr Emerson & it is a very charming old-fashioned trait in America to call their great writers long afterwards as "Mr". For instance they will still speak of "Mr Lincoln"!

I am so thrilled you enjoyed *my* Culture-Book. *That* & my Owen Glyn Dwr romance are the only 2 books I've ever had any royalties from, *after the first advance*! So I can tell you I know something about Publishers and they are *all* alike – save that Jewish ones are more civil & have more respect for the Vanity of Authors than the Gentile ones but not more anxiety to fill their wallets! I *do* thank you for Rees's *Adfeilion* which I have carefully inserted in a shelf just above my head between "Arabia Deserta" a good place to find Ruins!& poor *Mr* Longfellow's Poems; so they won't be disturbed by any *excavation* till I've done Rabelais but that I fear won't be till the middle of the Spring as I shan't have done the translation till next week & then & then only shall I really be off on the part that's easier to me. The text – "testun" – all in order & the old Pregethwr in (I hope!) his "hwyl". Yes I can see from the Rhestr fer o lyfrau just exactly what we're up against and what sort of bird we're "potting at" from Eric Gill to Spengler! & above all my old sweet enemy *Berdyaev* who, personally, I rejoice to hear, is still *safe & alive* near Paris. You & I are on the side of the Poet Shelley in these matters & as I am even now discovering, of Rabelais too! In fact the whole point of view was summed up by Pius XII in his recent Xmas broadcast. Well good luck.

Yrs as ever

John.

But *do try* to stick to the "John" now the ice is broken!

J.C.P. had asked me to send him a copy of Mr Alwyn D. Rees's small book *Adfeilion* (= Ruins), my notice of which he had read in *Y Cymro*.

Rhestr fer o lyfrau = A short list of books. *Pregethwr* = preacher.

12

7 Cae Coed / Corwen / Merionethshire / N. Wales
May 3 1944

My dear Iorwerth

Here is an extremely nice point for you to settle for I leave it entirely in your hands. Our friend Mr Evan Roberts of Llandderfel – & I am so vexed at their not giving him the proper Civil List Pension he so thoroughly – no one more – deserves – tells me that you – *what* a good friend you are to both him & me – are now helping him to try for a *Grant* from the Royal Literary Fund. He tells me he has officially enough support – you know? – sufficient *letters* from his admirers like ourselves – only 3 being called for – may be only 2 – but that it w^d. be nice – & I entirely agree – if I w^d. add my word to the others. Well! I had just finished doing so – *as here enclosed* – when the following consideration occurred to me rather forcibly. I have myself – & *well* I needed it! for I had come down to fewer pounds than you'd believe I confessed to it – received, thro' the good help of my family's old friend Mr Louis U. Wilkinson and others – a grant from the Literary Fund for £100. It is of course an outrageous thing – & exactly the sort of situation that proves the need here of a *Secretary of State* that your ancient friend John Powys should get a hundred pounds from the Fund that refuses to give a sou to friend Evan R. But now I expect you see what I mean by my hesitation over the wise diplomacy, purely from the view-point of the *success* of the appeal to this Fund on our friend's behalf of *my* letter being sent? Doesn't it look a *little* bit as if I . . . a neighbour & friend of E.R. *nudged* him *knowingly* – indicating with a motion of my thumb the direction in which – like an old fox passing the word to *another, not quite* so old, *fox* – a *wonderful Hen-Roost* was to be found? Well! my dear Iorwerth I leave it to you to tear up & burn the enclosed letter if you think there's truth in my *second thought* or to return it, *for Phyllis to type*, if you think I am being too fantastic in my apprehensions. What E.R. says is this: "Os carech chwithau roddi llythyr i fynd gyda'r ffurflen cais . . . a'i deipio a'i anfon yma i mi gan nodi eich adnabyddiaeth ohonof ac o'm gwerth hefyd. Carwn i'ch enw chwi fod ymhlith fy nghefnogwyr eiddgar". I *don't mind at all* your telling our friend about *my* grant; indeed I fancy I *did* hint at it to him but it seemed mean – you know? – to make much – tho' it was indeed a good deal, I can tell you, *to me*! – of *my finding* the "hidden pirate's treasure" that poor old crippled Evan had *missed*!

Alas! Since she lives in a *Banned Area* & both our younger sister Catherine Philippa, and Miss Alyse Gregory Llewelyn's widow, are with her within 3 minutes of the edge of those cliffs – they are too unwilling for her to come here at this time for her visit to be a happy one – for we'd be scared she'd be stranded en route somewhere in all the "invasion" rush! So she has – & I agreed – put off her visit "till August or October" she says. Her visits depend in their dates so much upon *BEES* for she's a great one for this Virgilian sport & has God knows how many hives. But she's got her new Big Canvas ready & has sworn not to use it for any other purpose but the toothless phyzz of her eldest brother.

As soon as I've done my Rabelais (& I'm doing the exciting part now, & I can assure you I'm *in a mood* for the Retort to *Adfeilion* w^h. I have already *ridden round* so to say in my mind) I'll send you for your Cymro column & to be translated by yourself which will do me proud – I know it! – my review of Alwyn D. Rees.

Well I'll do whatever you think wisest over the enclosed letter!

Yrs as ever

John.

A letter, signed 'John Cowper Powys, M.A. Cantab.', supporting the appeal for a grant from the Royal Literary Fund for Mr Evan Roberts was enclosed with the above letter. I advised him to send it. The quotation from E.R. reads in translation: 'If you would wish to supply a letter to accompany the application form . . . And to type it and send it to me here noting your knowledge of me and of my value too. I would like your name to be amongst those of my ardent backers.'

The second paragraph refers to his sister Gertrude's proposed visit. In the letter he illustrated the 'toothless phyzz' with a sketch.

His last paragraph indicates his continued determination to counter Mr Alwyn Rees's theories concerning culture.

13

7 Cae Coed / Corwen / Merionethshire
May 10 1944

My dear Iorwerth

I am so glad you decided in favour of my sending this letter to help out his appeal. I'll send it off to him at once after signing it. It is very nice of you Iorwerth to speak as you do about my friends trying [to] get a *Civil List Pension* for *me!* But listen my dear friend & read mark & digest my words on this quite serious matter.

I do not wish any of my friends to start, in the goodness of their hearts, such an idea in my case. The reasons for my objection which is very final as far as I can see are of a family nature – you know the convolutions of all family & domestic affairs & I am sure with your tact & wide sympathies have frequently had to read *round* as well as *between* the lines of what your friends say! – and quite apart from my brother Theodore already having a Civil List Pension which was given him by Ramsay Macdonald – it wouldn't do at all – at least as I see my situation now for me to try – I mean for any friends to try – to get me this. You see the Civil List is a Public & National thing & quite different from the Literary Fund w^h. is *private & confidential!*

As to my article for the *Cymro*, by yourself to be translated, I shall enormously enjoy writing that, the second Rabelais is safe off to my literary agent *en route* to John Lane Bodley Head. I note it is to be *an article* not a *Review* and I think that is much better for it leaves me a much freer hand but at the same time the inspiration of it will be an attack on this whole defeatist pessimistic reactionary Faith – once for all Delivered – aristocratic – "the land–the family–and the church" – Apologia for Ortho[do]xy which all over the world has tried of late to side-track into a *petrified eternity* all the natural free progressive movement, of the human race. 'Tis a 1000 pities that Saunders Lewis should throw his undoubted genius on this side for he is so clever & so right, I think, in lots of the things he says. I read

Cwrs y Byd from beginning to end every week (save when the *eco[no]mics* get a bit dull to me or beyond me) & I am always entertained & often impressed but all the while aye! I know *so* well all the familiar Catholic arguments! But he *is* witty, there's no doubt of it & very clever ... & a very good debater. What "Adfeilion" says is very much the same only without quite such a *positive Catholic* element – or the Holy Mass among the Ruins you might say! But I agree with you from the bottom of my heart & so would Rabelais! In fact it'll be under the influence of Rabelais that I'll try my hand at some ideas on "The Nature of Culture" and say my say about this "*new aristocratism*"! God! I'll get after it my dear friend – for I know the line of its arguments – & how *Berdyaev*'s Theology and *Maritain*'s Theology and T. S. Eliot's criticism all work together and with these sly ones we now have *Mr Clive Staples Lewis of Magdalene Oxford* who knows such a hell of a lot – a bit too much! – about the *Devil*! and whose notion of Christianity is for human nature to be *liquidated out of us* & for Christ becoming a sort of *Devil of Love* to act as a species of Incubus or Vampire absolutely *obsessing* us! Aye! my hand *shakes with rage* to think of *this New Orthodoxy*!

I'd better stop I think or I'll be working myself up into a torrent of marginal *Odium Theologicum*!

Yr ever sincere John.

'*Cwrs y Byd*' was a weekly feature in *Y Faner* newspaper which for many years Mr Saunders Lewis wrote. In this letter J.C.P. used up all his margins, hence the reference in his last sentence.

14

7 Cae Coed / Corwen / Merionethshire / N. Wales
May 14 1944

My dear Iorwerth

Alas! I must have misled you over my sentence about the finishing of RABELAIS & my START on Diwylliant Gwerin. 'Twas only I couldn't resist snatching a rushed glance at our Master Ruins pamphlet & soon well! *very* soon saw that I was confronted there by the old Gang of Reactionaries Debunkers of All Possible Progress & my fighting-gland began to itch to get after this little book! But alas! my dear Iorwerth I have *not* yet got my Rabelais anything like ready to go off to Mr Pollinger my Agent in Bedford St. Strand.

What I've finished is:
1. The translation part – about a 20th of the whole!
2. The life of R.
3. The Religion of R. And now I've only plunged into
4. The Genius of R. & there will still have to be done a brief
5. Preface about Authorities and Versions & thanks to people who've helped me with Dictionaries and Reference Books etc etc etc not to speak of correcting the *type*, and so far only the Translation part & the life of R. *has been* typed!

But all the rest from now on should be *clear sailing* – but *I'll be pleased* if I get it done & safe off to Mr Pollinger ready for Mr Greenwood – the Bodley Head Man – *somewhere during July*.

God! I had no idea that there was this connection between Middleton Murry & S. Lewis! But aye! I am so glad you felt like that over *Clive Staple Lewis*. My word! But what an authority on Demonology the fellow is! He'd better take care or "They" 'll be send[ing] twenty thousand cartloads of horned devils to *larn him to be a student* of Devilry!

It is certainly very singular how the Plan of Campaign of the "Apologists" (and what a giving of the show away it is that they should use *that* particular word to describe themselves) is the same today – the physical fagots & thumb-screws excluded *here* anyway but not I daresay under Franco or S. Lewis' pet Salazar of Portugal. Don't bother to answer this scrawl. – The very 1st line of yours I ever read was some passage where you attacked S. Lewis' linking this country – Wales I mean – so exclusively to the Latins. Yrs as ever J.

Don't 'ee bother to reply for this is only an explanatory P.S.!!

In this letter J.C.P. is still concerned about the article which he had promised me for *Y Cymro*, and which I was to translate. In it he is still concerned, too, with Mr Alwyn Rees's *Adfeilion* and refers to him, jokingly, as 'Master Ruins'.

In Letter 13 (p. 28) he had referred to Mr Saunders Lewis's weekly notes ('*Cwrs y Byd*') in *Y Faner*, and in my reply I had commented on the similarity between many of the opinions there expressed by Mr Lewis and those appearing weekly from the pen of J. Middleton Murry in *Peace News*, of which Murry was then editor. Unlike the *Peace News* Murry, however, Mr Lewis was not a pacifist.

15

7 Cae Coed / Corwen Merioneth
July 18 1944

My dear Iorwerth

I must thank you without a second's delay for this perfectly wonderful & *very* beautiful *Quilt*. As to *that word* it represents, Phyllis tells me & she has heard of it from her childhood up in the "*Middle West*", one of the most *deep-rooted diversions distractions* & *oases* of art for the pleasure of art & for the *leaving of something behind* when the daily round & common task is *over* & so often the noblest women pass away & – well! save their descendants (no negligible "save"!) – & *nothing left behind*! But we had a quilt once and it is still in our garden for it is the *shroud* of our Black Dog whose love passed the love of any man or woman or child who ever lived. The old-fashioned Cult of Quilts I speak of *Patchwork Quilts* in America must come *from here* & is one more proof of how the influence of this country (I speak of the Principality) has accounted for so many of the very best aspects of the best American tradition. But this work done in "the hungry forties" a hundred years ago is as you so beautifully & nobly say *just as it ought to have been said.* God my dear Iorwerth you *are* the true head of our National Museum. I am monstrous proud of thee my friend. You are doing something really precious & you've never done better than in this brief account. 'Tis like in its directness Goethe's description of Leonardo's Last Supper in Milan. That lion *does* look "enquiringly" – with its great maned head on one side.

That essay of mine I let "Wales" have for the Summer Number was written directly we got here from America but I could not get it taken there so K[eidrych] R[hys] is most kindly doing his best with it. I revised very little only inserting *what is really a lie* that I wrote it *recently after 10 years*! I am still working at Rabelais as I have done now for 2 years but I have got "Adfeilion" squeezed in between "Diwylliant Cymru" & "Arabia Deserta" and I tell you it'll be the 1st thing i'll go at when I *have* done this book. Well I must get back to

Rabelais. My book begins with his life – then the story of the Four Books – I discard the Posthumous Fifth as a *forgery*. Then my translation of my favourite passages about a *twentieth* of the whole then the Genius of Rabelais and finally the religion of Rabelais which is very like yours and mine that is to say religion of *Progress* and of Faith in Progress & Humanity!

Yrs as ever f'annwyl gyfaill
John.

I had sent J.C.P. a copy of my illustrated note (*Man*, 1944, p. 71) describing a quilt in the National Museum of Wales Folk Collection (now in the Welsh Folk Museum). This exceptionally fine patchwork quilt, made by a James Williams of Wrexham during the years 1842–52, would be, I believed, of great interest to him, and so it proved. Wales, however, was not the only country which gave America its fine patchwork-quilt tradition.

His article in *Wales* (Summer 1944) was 'Wales and America', subsequently reprinted in his *Obstinate Cymric* (Carmarthen, 1947, pp. 55–69). The reader will note also that Powys is still obsessed with his intention to write in defence of Welsh folk culture. His final phrase = 'my dear friend'.

16

7 Cae Coed / Corwen / Merionethshire / N. Wales
July 19 1944

This is only a hurried P.S. – but I've just read with much agreement your words about the worst of these modern *poems that are no poems* in the *Cymro*. I've tried to say the same thing in my rambling & long-winded way in my long preface to 50 recent lyrics of Huw Menai which I have chosen out of a heap of unpublished or only newspaper published poetry. I am very fond of Huw & am a great admirer of him and am linked closely physically with him for he is a sufferer & a much worse one than I from his stomach. Think of it Iorwerth! that unfortunate man hardly has had a day without vomiting for 20 years & on his feet now with his stomach so wrong in his munitions-plant. And even yet the whole of his family of 8 boys and girls are not self-supporting. He is a victim of a peculiar sort of fate . . . & his repute too is a queer up & down thing. But I shall be so thankful if I can get or my literary agent can get this selection published. You'll be amused how my championship of Huw Menai takes very much your line – well! you'll be amused if the book's accepted. But I can't tell! My Dostoievsky book has been unpublished now for 2 years.

By the way I forgot to ask your opinion on this nice point. You recall the making of Blodeued [Blodeuedd] "ac yna y kymmeryssant wy blodeu y deri a blodeu y banadyl a blodeu yr *erwein*".* Now its about this *erwein* I am doubtful (or *erwain* it is in Spurrel). *Lady Guest makes it meadow-sweet* and in my Botany Book (C. H. Johns Sheldon Press) "meadow-sweet" is the name of "*spiraea ulmaria*". Now Spurrel agrees with Lady Guest and calls *erwain* "meadow-sweet". But my point is this, Iorwerth, Meadow-Sweet is only *just out* in *mid-July*. Its a late, yes, *very* late summer flower whereas as you know the flower of the oak and the flower of the broom come together in April

---

* 'And then they took the flowers of the oaks, the flowers of the broom and the flowers of the *erwein*.' From *Math vab Mathonwy*.

or *very early in May* 2 *months at least before meadow-sweet*!! I put my problem to Mrs Morgan and *she* says that she always thought meadow-sweet was what Johns calls "wild Beaked-Parsley" or *Chervil "chaerophyllum sylvestre"* which Johns calls "*one of our early spring flowers*" (April to May & June). But it certainly would seem that even Gwydion, & why by the way does Robert Graves in his essay on Taliessin spell Gwydion Gwdion . . . is there any authority for that odd spelling or is it a mistake? But even Gwydion could not make a girl out of flowers that Nature did not cause to blossom *at the same time*!

Yrs ever *John* quoting *Johns*!

P.P.S. I want you to keep my sister Marion's article on *Fans*.

The 'long preface' to which J.C.P. refers appeared in *The Simple Vision*: Poems by Huw Menai, with a Preface by John Cowper Powys (London: Chapman and Hall Ltd., 1945). It is a brilliant piece of literary criticism in which he rejects those followers of T. S. Eliot for their 'vigorous attempt not so much to burn volcanic lava in the kitchen as to feed the smoking crater with kitchen coal, so as first and last and above all to evoke smoke'. Eliot's 'The Wasteland', he maintains, 'with all its intellectual and even social snobbishness . . . strikes us as the inspired genius of a terrible, deadly and "unsquared" disillusionment', but his followers merely 'evoked smoke . . . dealing out riddles in place of revelation'.

Huw Menai was a Caernarvon man who 'emigrated' to the coalfield of south Wales, where through ill-health, unemployment and much else, he suffered much. A Welsh-speaking Welshman, he wrote only in English, and was one of the very few Welshmen in the present century who made a positive contribution to English poetry.

In the second part of his postscript, J.C.P. raises a 'nice point' not yet considered by Welsh scholars. The tale of the creation of Blodeuedd from flowers by Gwydion (told in 'Math son of Mathonwy' – see Jones, G. and T., *The Mabinogion* (London, 1949), p. 68) fascinated Powys. All translators of the tale render *erwain* as 'meadow-sweet', and it so appears in the new University of Wales Dictionary, *Geiriadur Prifysgol Cymru*. But the late Professor W. J. Gruffydd, in his *Math vab Mathonwy* (Cardiff, 1928), p. 250, adds a note that 'the usual name for *S. Ulmaria* in Caernarvonshire is *Brenhines y Weirglodd*, 'Queen of the Meadow'; cf. the French name *Reine des prés*.'

Robert Graves's 'Gwdion' is, of course, wrong: the form is Gwydion.

17

7 Cae Coed / Corwen / Merioneth / N. Wales
July 26 1944

No I have not got your Welsh House & I'd be overjoyed to have it but if this reaches you too late never mind for I shall not be able to post this till tomorrow Thursday & it may not reach you in time ere you set out for your holiday so well-deserved.

I have just read this very day your most exciting & effective review of "Anarchistiaeth". It certainly *must* be an extraordinary development of an *unexpected* aspect of peace propaganda! But while I follow every single word of *your* critical words animadverting upon this work I fail to get *the author's main theme & contention* . . . in other words I don't really get what principles or ideas he writes this little book to advocate – unless it be *nationalism* – and to advocate nationalism *as against reason & liberty* & all the rest, as you say, and as a gesture and a move *towards peace*, when we all know that nationalism is the chief cause of – well! *one* of the causes of! – *war* seems very odd. Do you know what I thought at first? That it was a genuine *Anarchist Pamphlet*, yes! *praise of Philosophical Anarchy* as likely to lead to peace! Certainly for my own part I am inclined to think that Bakunin & Kropotkin and even dear old Emma Goldman tho' *she* was a born belligerent if ever there was one! are much more favourable to Peace than *any* nationalistic government. In fact though I speak only as an ignorant layman in these things I should be tempted to say that the chief causes of war are *always governments*. Governments are so much wickeder than private people & they have to propagandize private people into their wicked schemes!

Yrs as ever
John.

The second (general) edition of my book *The Welsh House* appeared in 1944.

The Welsh booklet on Anarchism which I had reviewed was by (now Professor) J. Gwyn Griffiths, Swansea.

18

7 Cae Coed / Corwen

[undated, but August 1944]

My dear Iorwerth

How *very* thrilled am I to have this wonderful & most precious volume. No question the most valuable book that has appeared for half a century here. I couldn't afford just now to buy it so I w^d. never have had it if you hadn't given it to me like this. We are so excited here & so will my sister be when *she* comes in October to paint that Portrait to see a picture of Plas ucha Llangar Merionethshire which I can almost see from these windows & w^h. my sister sketched! We've often been upstairs into that roofed chamber you have this picture of here!

The only sad thing to me about this wonderful work is that the person who would I know have appreciated it more than anyone else perhaps in all Ynys Prydain *sef* my brother A. R. Powys the architect & Sec. of the Soc^{ty}. for saving old Buildings is not able to read it being in his grave under the little Dorset church he restored by the sale of an MSS of T. Hardy.

Well I must stop now.

Yrs *most gratefully*

John.

This letter acknowledges the receipt of a copy of *The Welsh House* (2nd edn., Liverpool, 1944). *Ynys Prydain sef* = 'the Isle of Britain, namely'.

19

7 Cae Coed / Corwen / Merionethshire / N. Wales
Oct 13 1944

My dear Iorwerth

Well! my sister has now painted the Portrait of me & in my own humble opinion save for a little one of our Father which she has given me & which we have hung under the Death-Mask of my brother Llewelyn whose ashes are still in Switzerland where he died I think this picture – O save too, perhaps, for one of our old Nurse, Emily Clare, – is the best portrait she's ever made. I am, & so is Phyllis, simply delighted with it – & so are all our friends – well! I say "all" – but this really means J. Redwood Anderson the poet from Hull who is now settled in the Square here at "Stores House" opposite the Glyn Dŵr Hotel and Mr & Mrs Morgan who came up one Sunday I think it was & we had a very happy evening with them till night and indeed till midnight! who so far are the only ones who have so far seen it. She has painted me *as I am* the larger part of the 24 hours of each day i.e. on my back on my couch with a board propped against my knees & my paper on the board to write – & we are – well! – *she* was when I showed it to her in triumph – thrilled to see how her treatment of my hands and fingers holding my pen resembles the *manner* in which Holbein painted *Erasmus* a picture-card of which (for 'tis the *Ideal Writer* on portraiture) I've got balanced on my shelves along with Walt Whitman. It's in profile (as the Erasmus is!) and has my book-case full of all my best Welsh books behind as the Background. The books are indistinguishable of course as *individuals* but the general colouring of the background suggests a golden reddish brown, old leather-bound folios & otherwise rather *battered* books. As Edgar Poe says "of forgotten lore". My "bust of Pallas" however is the death-mask of Llewelyn on the other wall which does not appear; nor does any Raven – though I *hear* them – & so did Gertrude – as we went up our lane up the mountain this morn.

Gertrude has been so fascinated by your Welsh House which is indeed my dear Iorwerth a masterpiece in its genre – and a very important & original genre too. She knows being an artist much more than I do about these things and has been on the lock-out for *long* houses or long low-shaped houses in every walk even fancying that Mr Esmor Davies' Farm near that new bridge over the Dee – [?] – those whitewashed sheds, that you see from far away over there, was an example – but I tell her the house there is quite *separate* & is a square tall mid-Victorian erection!

She's going up tomorrow to have tea with Mrs Goodman at Angharad where I expect she'll see some old implements as that good lady is a Tremendous collector of old farming things Redwood Anderson tells me. He by the way has been having a class for the Sais-visitors in Welsh & also in French for others & now is going to give WEA lectures in Corwen like the one you gave at Betws Gwerfyl Goch when Phyllis heard you & said she had never known before how the Welsh tongue sounded in a speech till she went to that discourse.

I am continually having such a lot of *different opinions* about Cymraeg Cymreig when *spoken* or *preached* and how differently it sounds from BBC talk in that tongue (when they give it to us!) and how completely different from what the language sounds *when spoken*. I can follow a French platform speech myself much better than – well! I can't follow this latter *at all*! – than I can French colloquial talk. But alas! I shall never be able to speak or to follow the spoken language of my fathers. I am too hopelessly un-musical. I can't *catch* the sound. But that I *am* "getting on" as we say with *reading* Cymraeg is proved by the fact that I read your un-signed "*Gwerinwr*" article last week without looking out one single word in B. Anwyl, Spurrell! But aye! Iorwerth I did & do so agree with every word of it especially with your last sentence "ac yn sicr bydd angen mawr yn y blynyddoedd sydd o'n blaen am wŷr sy'n credu mewn rhyddid i anghytuno". But I do so thoroughly agree with your view of the question Classic–Romantic and I rejoiced from the bottom of my heart at your strictures on *Jaques Barzun*. You wait, my friend, till I've done my Rabelais which is entirely defending your principles about life & religion, and then I'll give you something on *Adfeilion* to translate for your columns! But I've been interrupted by *nice people* with their – the most insidious & fatal of all! – interruptions & I've also had a "bout" caused (what a word "bout" is!) yes a "bout" of the old affliction caused by excitement of *nerves causing gastric acids to hurt* my weakest spots!

The Morgans – but I may have misunderstood them – seemed to feel as if it were not impossible that you might be coming this way for some purpose ere long – & if so I need not say how I long for you to see my sister's Picture of me & then you'll be able to consider its chances & merits & whether it is or not the sort of Barque to carry her & me & our gratitude to thee down over the horizon! I know that for myself I'm *quite satisfied* with it.

Yrs as ever

John Thy Faithful Friend.

Gertrude M. Powys had now completed the portrait (see Frontispiece) of her brother John, and his description of it, meticulously correct as it is, is of interest. The resemblance to the Erasmus portrait evidently pleased him, while his description of his books takes him to Edgar Allen Poe's study as described in 'The Raven', Llewelyn's death-mask being Poe's 'bust of Pallas'.

John Redwood Anderson, the Yorkshire poet, author of *The Human Dawn, The Vortex, Transvaluations, The Tower to Heaven, Paris Symphony, The Pursuit of Diarmuid and Graunia, Pillars to Remembrance, While the Fates Allow* and several other volumes of poems, was a schoolmaster who came during the Second World War to Corwen where he became a proficient Welsh speaker and writer.

J.C.P. was troubled about his own inability to speak and fully to comprehend spoken Welsh, as his paragraph about '*Cymraeg Cymreig*' (lit. 'Welsh Welsh'!) shows. He did not seem to realize that what he heard daily was the local dialect.

J.C.P. had read, without the aid of a dictionary, my article (*Y Cymro*, October 8, 1944) on certain aspects of the problem of Classicism and Romanticism, but he had evidently misread a passing reference to Jacques Barzun, Professor of History at Columbia University, for my only reference to his work, *Romanticism and the Modern Ego*, was that it was 'an enlightened discussion'. The translation of the passage from my article which Powys quotes reads: 'There will be great need in the years before us of men who believe in freedom to disagree'.

20

7 Cae Coed / Corwen / Merioneth / N. Wales
Oct 18 1944

My dear Iorwerth

Yes sure! I *do* really believe (but I am not artistic enough to be *sure*) that Gertrude's portrait *is* a Success! I am anyway inclined to think *she* was satisfied with it for I heard her distinctly utter the words "It's not too bad" – & you know what these artists are!

Your list of pictures already to be seen make me long to be a visitor *out of a frame* for I'd particularly be interested to see the countenance of W. J. Gruffydd. T. Gwynn Jones I *have* seen several times in pretty good newspaper reprints & like his look particularly but I have never seen any however poor of W. J. G. I shall also like to see when you yourself consent *there to be hung* how you are handled.

No I must have misunderstood what the Morgans said! Well, it can't be helped. We shall meet again some day – I'm sure *that* is writ in our stars! Yes my sister says she'd like well to send it on loan and so it shall be done and I will send it next month & let you know if the packing of it & carriage of it are beyond my purse and beyond the packers of our town when the moment comes. My sister says it ought to be framed – it is *not* a big picture – and she says she wonders if you or those concerned or those you are in the habit of employing for such tasks would kindly *frame* it; for as I say it is *not* a large picture and let her have, through me, the bill for this, so that both picture and frame would be hers. But since it will be probably our local coffin-maker – (I begin to catch the rumour here of a situation similar *to the taste* of "our fore-father Donne" in "thik little job"!) – who will pack it here – luckily I shall be able to ask our new Corwen Permanent Sais Refugee from Sais impercipience Mr J. Redwood Anderson the poet who was brought up in Brussels till (damn! I can't spell the name) he was twenty & is an authority on art & on *transporting* art, as I expect people have had to learn to be in Europe of late! &

who has now settled in our Corwen Square at *"Stores" House* (a name he has discovered belonging to some House or other in almost all the towns round here) where *Miss Humphreys* a *very* nice lady who couldn't be better adapted to be the guard & landlady of an exiled homeless poet is making him "feel at home" for the first time for many a year tho' he is over 60 – luckily therefore, as I began to say, I shall be able or our coffin-maker who is a near relative of Miss Humphreys will be able to ask Mr Anderson's advice as to *how* to pack a picture unframed on canvas like this – but if we die in too great numbers in Corwen during the end of this month and the beginning of Nov and since it will be as I was saying some pages back I fear for I'm a scandalous deboucher & digresser – in fact *all* (I say all!) my best inspirations are debouchings & digressions – & *like you* if I depended on the *narrow way* according to the stablished orthodox "Unities" of Transport & Travel, I'd never, any more than you, have an illuminating word to say on such topics! Since it will be upon a digressing & *historical* novelist's initiative and a coffin-maker performance under a poet's instruction it may be *several weeks* ere this Portrait reach you! & shall I, when it *is* sent off (sometime in November) & by *luggage train*, I take it, eh? – send it addressed to you at the Department of Folk Culture?? or how shall I have it addressed??? *Don't forget* to answer *this* when you *next write* but no hurry! No hurry in answering, so don't bother to write till a really leisurely moment. Duw! but I am glad your *Clocks* and their *Makers* are ready for printing and that you are revising your Folk Crafts Guide. Long may you live & may you complete all your most cherished projects; long after your admirer John is dust and ashes.

Yrs as ever

John.

You see Gertrude where she lives has great difficulty over *frames* & all the ones she has are now "engaged" & I doubt if even Redwood A. could direct the making of one here or near here.

This is the first of several letters relating the tale of sending J.C.P.'s portrait – a small painting 21 × 17 inches – from Corwen to Cardiff.

The late Sir Leonard Twiston-Davies had asked me how best he could assist in the development of the National Museum of Wales. I had made a number of suggestions, all of which he adopted. One was that he should initiate a scheme for securing portraits of eminent living Welshmen. Kind and generous as he always was in such matters (he had, some years previously, donated £500 to initiate the establishment of a department of folk-life studies) he now expressed his willingness to pay several artists – Morse Brown, Powys Evans and Evan Walters – to produce portraits of such living Welshmen if I advised him about the persons who should be chosen. Not all of them accepted the invitation (the poet Robert Williams Parry was one of these notable exceptions, much to my sorrow). But through Sir Leonard's generosity, the Museum obtained a series of portraits of outstanding twentieth-century Welshmen. Years later, when I had come to know J.C.P., I felt that he, too, should be represented.

John Donne (like William Cowper) was one of J.C.P.'s 'forefathers' (see Louis Marlow, *Welsh Ambassadors*, p. 5).

The books referred to in the last paragraph were two National Museum publications:

Clock and Watch Makers in Wales (Cardiff, 1945; 2nd edn., 1960).

Welsh Folk Crafts and Industries (Cardiff, 1945, 2nd edn.).

21

7 Cae Coed / Corwen / Merioneth
Oct 25 1944

My dear Iorwerth

The canvas is only 21 inches by 17. But my Phyllis thinks she *may* be able to discover a box suitable for it . . . & we still have friend Redwood Anderson who knows a lot about these things to fall back upon not to speak of our excellent maker of Coffins for Corwen in whose sister's house in the Square the said R. Anderson our poet from Yorkshire has his abode! So we have other strings to our bow & I'll write to my sister about the frame – yes it w^d. be put in *her* name – as the owner of it. I know R. Anderson recently found somebody in Wrexham to frame a pretty large old map for his room; so maybe I could get a frame as near as that. Anyway I'll write to my sister about it. So don't 'ee bother anymore till I tell you what *she* says! I note what you said about Passenger Trains if over 16 lbs. O no I *well* understood how rushed you are. But I'll give you my dear Iorwerth for future use my sister Gertrude's address. It is as follows:

Miss Gertrude Mary Powys, "Chydyok", East Chaldon, Dorchester, Dorset. *What* a comfort your clear hand is & *how* rare in my other friends!

Yrs as ever

John.

P.S. I note the box is to be eventually addressed to you at your Museum address.

22

7 Cae Coed / Corwen / Merioneth / N. Wales
Nov 10 1944

My dear Iorwerth

Well! you'll be ready to sympathize with me I know in my pleasure at learning that a friend of my sister's *has found* the right kind of frame in London (namely a thick old-fashioned *gilded* one I *hope*, tho' my sister doesn't say that!) but at any rate a *good* frame *has* been found in London and in a week [or] so for it has to be tinkered up a bit – will arrive here when I will put the picture into it with the help of our good neighbour a skilful man of his hands & the advice of Poet Anderson who was brought up in Brussells and had as his teacher in art etc no other than the great Belgian–Flemish Poet Vaerharen I can't spell his name but you'll know of him I expect. I've only seen extracts from him in anthologies of modern poetry but I have a sort of notion he was a species of Belgian Walt Whitman – more of the former element in him than the latter no doubt, but – still! The advice, I say, of Anderson as to packing it again when it *is* framed! But *all moves slowly everywhere* as this hard and cruel winter begins for all the world, – but the picture *will* I believe *finally* arrive & it shall be addressed to you at the Museum. Then all you'll have to do will be to have it unpacked & the *case* I presume sent back either to London or to my sister – I must ask her *that* little point – for I daresay proper cases for pictures are not to be picked up in any shop these days.

I think I really shall get my revision & correcting of the typed version of my Rabelais-book by January 1st & into the Publisher's hands – *& then* I'll celebrate & in good how ha? the "New Age", the *Aquarian zodiacal one* according to "Old Moore" by criticising Adfeilion for your translation & column in *Cymro*. I was so greatly interested to hear about your Aberystwyth visit & Gwyn Jones & Dr T. Gwynn Jones and I am very pleased to hear this latter looked fit although older. But the war has made us all older – men *and* women both –

especially the latter. No I've *never* met that J. W. Jones of Blaenau Ffestiniog – I w^d. dearly like to do so. I follow with the utmost sympathy your excellent campaign against orthodoxy! Well I must stop & get back to my "guerilla" or "partisan" attack on the same enemy only more indirectly through the great Heretic Rabelais!

Yrs as ever

John.

Thomas Gwynn Jones (1871–1949) was the greatest poet and literary figure of the twentieth century (and probably of all time) in Wales. The son of a Denbighshire farmer, he did not receive a University education but at an early age became a journalist. His health broke down, and during the First World War he was a member of the staff of the National Library of Wales. In 1919 he was made Professor of Welsh Literature at the University College of Wales, Aberystwyth. His succession of great poems – *Ymadawiad Arthur, Gwlad y Bryniau, Tir na n-og, Broseliawnd, Anatiomaros, Madog, Argoed, Gwlad Hud, Cynddilig* — his translations of Goethe's *Faust*, of *Macbeth*, and of Irish and Greek poems, his biographies, novels and plays, together with his many works on the history of Welsh literature, entitled him, in the opinion of many, to be nominated for the Nobel Prize, but he firmly declined to be so nominated. His poems and creative prose writings were published in a definitive six-volume edition. He received honorary doctorates from the Universities of Ireland and Wales.

23

7 Cae Coed / Corwen / Merionethshire
Dec 5 1944

Just a line my dear Iorwerth enclosing my sister's note. I have not read it but I gather from her that she trusts it will be possible for your people at the Museum to keep in the "cellarage" or whatever store-room for such lumber may exist *the wooden case* in which I hope ere long – that is as soon as our carpenter here (who lives near Anthropos' "Pentre Gwyn"!) can be induced to turn up to get the Picture into its Frame which is now safe here with us and is quite a nice solid gilded one, though the *moulding* is not altogether as deep as I *could* have desired – however! it'll suffice – it'll serve – though it *isn't* "as deep as a church porch"!

But I'll do just what you said to do & send it by Passenger Train addressed to you at the Museum.

I'm now teased & vexed to find that I can't at once in these two weeks before Xmas plunge into my little *anti-Adfeilion* article for you to translate for "Y Cymro" but *by* Xmas, *between* Xmas and Jan 1st I hope to get at it. But now that I've finished my Rabelais & got it off I am to my vexation confronted with the task of cutting into chapters which means a bit of changing & tinkering my short book on Dostoievsky which Staples & Staples have now given up & the Bodley Head want it – but want also these afforesaid tinkerings! I am longing to get back to my long Historical Romance one quarter already begun of that mysterious epoch when a Romancer can Romanticize about Ynys Prydein to his heart's content – 50 years *after* St Patrick's confession and 50 years *before* Gildas, i.e. *500* A.D.! But I'm going to fight shy I tell you of the Knights of the Graal. For my romance is *more realistic* than *that* comes to!

Well – good luck! Gertrude's address is Miss Powys Chydyok East Chaldon Dorchester Dorset. & don't ee bother to acknowledge this scrawl of mine – I know how busy you are.

Yrs ever

John.

Robert David Rowland (1853?–1944) was a Calvinistic Methodist minister who, under the pen-name 'Anthropos', published over twenty volumes of verse and essays. His best work was as an essayist. One of his most popular works was *Y Pentre Gwyn*, referred to here by J.C.P.

In this letter, J.C.P. refers for the first time to the 'long historical romance' which became *Porius*. In Letter 1 (1937) he wrote: 'Yes by Heaven I think your hint for a *future* romance is splendid.' This was in answer to my suggestion for a romance set in the Dark Ages. He chose *c*. A.D. 500 for the purpose.

24

7 Cae Coed / Corwen / Merioneth
Dec 14 1944

My dear Iorwerth

I am so glad you like the Picture. It is such a relief it is safe in your hands & will reach now its glorious pro-tem destination & haven. But its Future is on the *lap* or *knees* note we don't say laps so it's either the Great Mother the Goddess of Bloodless Offerings of fruit & flowers *or* it's just the common & garden *male gods* snuffing up their bullocks' blood in hecatombs! but any way as old Hardy said to me when the last war was over my calling up "it's on the lap" he said, (making them epicene or hermaphrodite!) "of the gods" giving them an apron between them! But its future (this admirable Portrait's I mean!) is dependent on my sister to whom it belongs – and I think it's on *the cards* – the *tarot* ones maybe w^h. the gypsies kept & where Phoenicia enters – that after a decent & honourable while of biding in that noble court of the Rulers of the South she'll be wanting it back in Wessex. I really cannot tell – but meanwhile here's luck to you! & I pray your Clock speech *satisfied* you in every way. We speakers are so rarely satisfied with ourselves.

Yrs ever
John.

25

7 Cae Coed / Corwen / Merionethshire / N. Wales
March 1 Dewi Sant 1945

My dear Iorwerth

I do thank you so much for this most fascinating clock-making paper & I want also to tell you how greatly I liked every word of your most suggestive article (or review) of last week on those essays by Mr Davies – especially with regard to political parties etc. I certainly do agree *with all you say* in your "Y Cymro" column though here & there I'd go just a bit further in the direction of re-fashioning our ideals & changing our customs and habits of thought. But I am on your side – like a light-armed skirmisher as it were!

Well! I've finished my own essay *originally inspired* by my agreement with your strictures on that gloomy *Spengler*-dominated book of Alwyn D. Rees called "Adfeilion". There's too much in it of that niggardly, finicky & gingerly & superiorly *designed de-bunking* such as T. S. Eliot started the fashion for, for my – well! not my easy-going temperament exactly, but my slap-dash *healthily resilient* temperament to stand! This essay of mine I have entitled

Pair Dadeni

or

The Cauldron of Rebirth

and I'm sending the MSS to Dorchester today to get it typed – so I shall have more than one copy. It'll be back in a week I expect or ten days any way; but I should *think* I'll be able to be posting it off to you in ten days if not before. It'll be *too long* I expect as it is. In fact I am sure it will. But you could if so it hit your humour *translate* (just as you often quote in your reviews from books) *as much of it* (selecting passages that suited you best) as you could use; and either joining them up by remarks of your own or just letting them run on consecutively – only with . . . dots to fill the gaps between the paragraphs selected? Don't you think so?

What I want to do with this essay which is *so far* the furthest I've dared to go in the direction of *prophesying*! and I have been following this line of darogan-ing (so to say) or brudio-ing in my two-year-and-a-half Book on Rabelais & in the much shorter & much less thorough book on Dostoievsky – could there be a greater contrast? – but I've managed to *give* them both (or *find* in both) a certain *gogwydd* in the direction of my own secret wishes I expect! Both these books are I expect being *pruned* by Publishers expert-"readers" & then there'll be more labour for Master John! But I really have summarized the most exciting – I won't presume to say the "truest" – portions of these rather daring "proffwydoliaethau" in this essay – and as I have begun to say what I want to do with it *after* you have translated what of it or if you preferred just quoted from it but I would myself be by far more interested if it weren't too much trouble for you – & you with so much on your hands of both public and private work – in your translating it or what of it you had space for & cared to use – well! what I hope to do with it *then* after you've used what you want – (and of course if you *do* translate some of it there'll be *no* hurry . . . you can use it at any date that suits your convenience & Y Cymro's convenience) – is to let Keidrych Rhys have it as the 8th essay – he's already got 7 – on Welsh subjects for a little book in his DRUID Press . . . a book which already includes my essay on *James Joyce's* "*Finnigan's Wake*' or of what I understand of it & I daresay a *bit* I *don't* understand too for there's a kind of piquant & tempting *mental snobbishness* in pretending to understand an obscure modern author which is far worse than blood-snobbishness – & only *not* – in my casuistical opinion – *quite* as bad as *spiritual* snobbishness! – what I understand of it & *what I don't* I *like* – for you can like what you don't understand – (as I know well in my readings in the Welsh language very often!) – a lot better than "*Ulysses*".

Will this be *O.K.*, my friend, from the point of view of *Y Cymro*?

The young man who first printed that Joyce essay in his "*Modern Reading*" No. 7 was Reginald Moore. Well! the *only* one whose [*sic*] printed it for I doubt (but I have no idea – for I never bother publishers or editors with unnecessarily [*sic*] fussiness –) whether so far the Druid Press has begun printing this little book – & I daresay K. Rhys is waiting even now impatiently for his promised 8th essay which *I've written to him you were to see first for translation for Y Cymro*.

I've never met Keidrych Rhys though I've got his anthology. But as I have explained at length in my most long-winded & serpentine manner in my essay to a volume of my friend Huw Menai's new poems soon to appear published by Chapman & Hall – I am *not* good at obscure modern poetry, in these things I'm *old-fashioned*. In fact in *Poetry* I'm a Tory, whereas (tho' I am an *odd* Tory since my favourite poet is Walt Whitman) whereas in philosophy & morals & social questions I'm the extreme opposite of a Tory!

And the same Reginald Moore whose address is – I've never met *him* either but we have a mutual friend in James Hanley who now lives at *Llanfechain* – but R. Moore's address is Gelli Cottage, *Llansantffraid*. He's written to me lately asking for some articles for his publications which are things like "*Modern Reading*" – paper-backed periodicals, you know the edition? but I told him I only had *this* one & that you were going to have the 1st handling of for translation for Y Cymro; but I said if *his* periodical could be worked in *before* Rhys' *book* I'd no objection to killing 2 birds with one stone! But he seems to think as far as I can gather from his words that that's impossible. So apparently the Sais is out of it & I've yourself & Rhys alone on this Essay's programme.

No hurry about replying my friend for at the moment my Pair Dadeni is only just being conveyed to Durnovaria for typing.

Yrs as ever

John.

This long letter well illustrates J.C.P.'s 'serpentine manner' of writing. The 'Mr Davies' referred to was then Professor Emlyn Davies of the Baptist Theological College, Cardiff, whose book *Cymru: Chwe Astudiaeth* (= Wales: six studies) the Student Christian Movement had published.

Darogan = to prognosticate; *brudio* = to divine; *proffwydoliaethau* = prophesyings; *gogwydd* = trend.

26

7 Cae Coed / Corwen / Merionethshire
March 9, 1945

My dear Iorwerth

I am so interested in your being thrilled by the works of Albert Schweitzer for I was absolutely fascinated by the "Profile" of him – with a picture and brief sketch of his life & work that appeared in the *Observer* some months ago – in the autumn I fancy it was. I felt the very greatest attraction to him & admiration for him then – even to meditating cutting his history out and pinning it up on my bookshelf! But I've never read one single line of him nor have ever heard mention of him before I saw that notice in The Observer.

I have got some sort of superficial *"line" on* (or ought we to say "lien" on? I never know!) the orthodox apologists.

1. English Church. The writer of Mystery-Thriller Clive Staple Lewis of Magdalene Oxford.

2. Roman Church. Maritain.

3. Lutheran etc., etc. R. Neibhuhur damn I can't remember where that "h" or that "u" or any of the other vowels come & I gave away my volume of him to our Rector on leaving for Abergele. Prof R. Niebuhr – *that begins* to look better! I go by *look*, never ear – (& so you *have* to with English!) (of the New York Protestant Seminary) and of course the one of these orthodox champions (if *he* can be called so) representing the Greek Church my favourite far of the lot –*sef*– Berdyaev of whom I heard first from *Dorothy M. Richardson* the novelist who lent us one of his volumes – and since then I've [*word deleted*] I was going to say got him like you did *this* one but that wouldn't be true for an Irish boy (whose Dad's a Roman Catholic Master in a school near Bridgend) and who's now in the Camel Corps in Somali-land sent me or ordered for me his Complete Works, the best of which to me is the latest called "Slavery" or something, I forget exactly. For myself – I mean in my private secret life – I am a great one for *praying* for I pray very hard

for *definite sufferers* both human and sub-human and I do so (as a Roman Catholic would) only particular stones and stumps and rocks & streams are so to say my "beads".

But my quarrel with the Catholic Church and the Greek Church and the Anglican Church and with all the Nonconformists too is hopelessly temperamental instructive intuitive & both super- & sub-rational and is exactly the same quarrel I have with the rationalists and with the vivisectory scientists. – In plain words in spite of an almost morbidly Christian conscience which I have to restrain as I restrain my vices purely for common sense reasons of legitimate self preservation and sanity – my attitude to all these questions is essentially agnostic and heathen & indeed *pluralistic* as opposed to *monism* of every sort, the sort of pluralism W. James wrote of – tho' they tell me Whitehead is a pluralist; but I lack the *brain* to cope with *him*! My pluralism is a temperamental intuitive preference for the Many over the One – and for a certain Anarchy in things over One Cosmos and one God & One Christ. I like absolutely free speculation in these things and *I like to question* not only the *existence* of God – the *desirability* of following Christ – the moral order, like my brother Llewelyn. *The only thing* w^h. I feel I *know* to be evil wicked and wrong is *direct mental & physical cruelty* – the value of the Family etc etc etc. Like you, I reluct at the tyranny of the Church as well as at the tyranny of the new totalitarian State. – But it is destined to come I think and we libertarians were wise to try and humanize it ere *and as* it comes! But nobody will be able to stop it! And it'll be agreeable to see it sweep away *Class Privilege* etc etc etc. I shall enjoy *that* part of it & I'm sure you will too. Yes, I fear we shall have to pay the price; but it'll be a malicious pleasure to see the *great ones* pay it as well as the rest of us!

Well I shall be now sending you the typed copy of my Essay on all these matters entitled Pair Dadeni or Cauldron of Rebirth. I'll get it off to you on Monday March 12 I expect. Oh yes my friend but there is one thing I must insist on (for here comes in my Categorical Imperative!) I *do not want to appear to know more Welsh* than I do. I've been studying it for 10 years and shall die without being able to *speak* a word [of] it or to follow a word when spoken – It's my lack of ear. I am the same with French that I can read about as easily as I can read Welsh but cannot *write* a grammatical sentence or *any* presentable sentence without hours of labour. It takes me a whole day to write a letter in Welsh. This is because I am (& always have been) *just hopeless* over syntax & grammar. What I would like you to say is that while I can read the language I lack the musical ear to speak it and am too hopeless in grammar to ever write it *I am afraid*. So I implore you, my dear friend, to explain this in a brief sentence and to say you are translating it. But I wish you would also say that I am a fanatical adherent of the language and *would never – unless I could get a translator* – send an English contribution to a Welsh paper or periodical. I am a fanatical and humble *reader* of real Welsh writers who write in Welsh like yourself & your friends. I was puzzled by Saunders Lewis saying the Anglo–English [*sic* = -Welsh] poetry was better than the *real* Welsh poetry. I longed to have made cuttings of the best Welsh poems I've read in Y Faner.

Well I must stop! But *please* Iorwerth *say* that it is translated because I lack the power yet. But also perhaps say too that I am a fanatic on the point of *keeping English out of a Welsh paper* save in quotations when indispenable of course. Yes I reverence the language too much and would like to be able to write in it too well to bear the idea of people *thinking I am further advanced in it than I really am. One day* perhaps! – I *may achieve it.* But I *doubt* it.

This essay is 8804 words so it's far too long but you will soon decide what of it to translate.

This letter is unsigned. It is amazing that J.C.P. had 'never heard' of Albert Schweitzer until he read a chance profile of him in 1944.

All lovers of the Welsh language will note his 'fanaticism' for it.

27

Corwen

March 22 / 1945

Only a scrawl to return this *most fascinating* tale of the life of Schweitzer, with 1000 thanks. Also to express my great gratitude for your humoring me so considerately & gently about that punctilious point of – what shall I say? – the *scrupulosity* of an industrious efrydydd who is not an ysgolhaig. Don't 'ee worry about being literal or too exact in your translation of whatever pieces you've room for. The patching the quotations together to make it continuous might be the devil of a job to anyone who didn't think along pretty well (with only a *bit* more stress on Xtianity perhaps) the same lines. But you I know do with only the inevitable differences of being *you Iorwerth* – & *I* yr grateful friend.

John.

The 'tale' returned was a study of Schweitzer as a 'leader of theological thought' by Principal W. B. Selbie, D.D., Oxford.

Efrydydd = student; *ysgolhaig* = scholar.

28

7 Cae Coed / Corwen / Merioneth / N. Wales
Friday April 13 1945

Unlucky though Friday 13 *might* appear, 'tis lucky to me this day! – for I just, my dear kind amazingly clever friend, read your lovely version of my article in "Y Cymro". I was simply thrilled by it my dear Iorwerth. I tell you I almost cried with pleasure at the way you'd made my rather *peculiar kind* of rhetoric fall into the perfect rhythm of the tongue of my fathers. It's a little triumph of translation and transliteration and how you did it I *cannot* conceive! God! you're a *real* master at this job of writing, so hard to some! Sentence after sentence you turned so easily and you emphasized exactly the passages I hoped you would – I tell you again I don't know *how* you did it. O I pray it didn't prove a bother to you or take too much of your time for well I know how rushed & crowded your life is.

But I tell you if the pleasure it gave me could be put in a little Box of Precious Ointment and sent off to you by Registered Post it w^d. scent the whole of 29 Lôn y Dail of Riwbina! I shall never forget your kindness Iorwerth in doing this.

Don't bother to acknowledge this scrawl for it is only thanks all thanks & nothing but wonder – and thanks.

Yrs as ever

John.

At last, the essay *Y Pair Dadeni* had been written, and a part translated and published in *Y Cymro*, April 13, 1945. Its subject had obsessed J.C.P. ever since he had read my notice of Mr Alwyn D. Rees's 56-page booklet *Adfeilion* in August 1943. It is his hopeful answer to what he had called 'gloomy Spenglerism'. I have no doubt, however, that if J.C.P. were alive now he would be the first to acclaim Mr Rees's distinguished contribution throughout the years to the cause of the Welsh language and its culture.

29

7 Cae Coed / Corwen / Merionethshire
April 19 1945

My dear Iorwerth

Yes *sure*! *By all* means keep that typed copy for I've got the carbon which I shall be sending soon to Keidrych Rhys as soon as I know he's at his London Address but "it said" somewhere that he was going on an excursion to the Welsh Forces at the Front ... I presume to get some data for his next issue of "Wales" but I have no idea whether this is true or not.

But if by an evil chance this carbon copy gets lost in its attempts to arrive on the Desk of Mr. K. Rhys I'll send you an S.O.S. begging for the original type-script *but* when K. Rhys has got it safely & included it in his "Druidical" Publications I'll let you know that all's O.K.

Duw! It shows what a hopeless one I am at scholarship that I never noticed that sentence which went wrong by the omission of a line ... even now as I read "darganfyddaf I discover yn barhaus constantly Socrateses sy'n llawn who are full o'r anwadalu dynol rhy ddynol of the human too human waverings a geir yng nghydwybod a synnwyr cyffredin naturiol dyn of conscience & thought common to the natural man" – the fault escapes me!

But it's my weakness in syntax & grammar that is my obstacle. I'm getting quite a *good vocabulary* you know, Iorwerth, but *no syntax no grammar* & *absolutely no ear*!

Don't you bother, f'annwyl Gyfaill, to answer *this* scrawl. It is more & more wonderful to see how many strings you have to your bow.

Yrs as ever
John.

I had apologized to J.C.P. that the printer's omission of a word (not 'a line') had rendered a sentence in my translation of his essay meaningless. In this letter (third paragraph) he spells out the sentence in Welsh and English, and the fault escaped him. But he had misread 'Socrateses' for *Socrataidd*; the word *ddadleuon* had been omitted (*dadleuon Socrataidd* = Socratic debates.)

of old essays —
well! of essays writ in
these last 13 years —
— since Phyllis & I and
her mother & aunt
settled down here
in this excellent
couple of next-door little new houses
was to appear — quite
a long while ago last & was but
I fancy it was —
when I thought on publication was
imminent & there was no
time for delay I was seized
with a desire to write hurriedly
quickly and so to say at
one breath a complete
new & fresh essay! I am
as I've often told you I expect a lecturer
story-teller, preacher, & speaker, (even an orator
first, & a writer secondly & the
not being an artist I don't worry a
punctuation or even any syntax or
take little or take no interest in writing or
mine once they've been
So to make this little book — for
as with most of my books I
publisher invent the title &
rather like this odd one
tho' maybe it should
been Cyprus an

The first and last leaves of a letter written by

Sunday night
Nov 16
1947
7 Cae Coed
Corwen

My dear Iorwerth

Just a line to tell you only 2 things!

But this scrawl needs no reply, for you are a very old friend & I am an ancient Pensioner at Leisure so it'll only

30

7 Cae Coed / Corwen / Merioneth
April 25 1945

My dear Iorwerth

Damn! I wrote at once in reply to your most kind letter of the 16th & lo & behold! on my way to post it I went through a wood above the road rail & river by a forester's "drove" – ending in a sort of mossy rocky precipice with a cave I wanted to experiment with (I mean *in*!) in view of my Romance of Corwen in 499 A.D. into which I am now plunged to the neglect of many things and in which I now float & swim & rest on its coral-reef and its isles in perilous seas and when I reach the port *there* were the 2 *other* letters which I carried in my basket for bread & buns – fool! not to have put them into an inner pocket! – and the 3rd the one to thee gone! I went next day to hunt but for an *Ordivicean* I can't spell! to be writing to another Ordivician (if that's the word!) in the land of those savage Silurians was too much for the tutelary geniuses of this Border Land & I could *not* find it! In it I'd said *by all means – it's nice of you to want to keep* your (I mean my) type-script used by you so well! For I've heard from Rhys that he's on the job down there in Carmarthen & I'm to send him the carbon as I promised for his "Druid Press" Edition of 7 sketches (more or less connected) to w^h. as an 8th this Dadeni will be added. I also said – may it be of interest to our North-Eastern Border *elementals* who clearly disapprove of our having anything to do with these South-Westerners! – that I was so bad a linguist that hunt as I might for that Socrates mistake of the Printer – it escaped me. But never mind that now, Iorwerth my friend. And don't trouble to answer *this* – even if a forester found my 1st one & posted it! I *was* so proud of the look of my article in the oldest European language!

Yrs as ever
John.

No reply to this needed.

'A forester' had obviously found Letter 29 and posted it.

31

7 Cae Coed / Corwen / Merionethshire / N. Wales
July 20 1945

F'annwyl Iorwerth

No no! you know I always respect your labours far too much *ever* to want you to write till the coast is quite clear or you have a day to rest on your oars.

What a disappointment it is to me to learn that the limitations on petrol – but I *am* so glad for your sake my dear Iorwerth you've *got* your car in action again – will mean you can't visit Corwen. For no! alas! I've got fixed in a hopeless *groove* (I was saying *grove*!) not *entirely* the malingering of a Valetudinarian Hermit but I daresay not *perfectly* free from that egotistical weakness – over any sort of journey by car or by bus or by rail *even the shortest*. I *just get on* (at least that's how, as these devils say, I "rationalize" my cowardice & selfishness & fear of life!) with this fixed régime of walking for 2 hours before breakfast on an absolutely empty stomach. I combine this with doing some of the marketing for our two little houses for as you know Phyllis's aged mother & aunt live next door at No 8 – and on Thursdays & Sundays with getting the sticks or fire-wood or *"kindling"* as we used to say in New York for our two kitchens! This last is no mean undertaking for as I grow more & more like Wordsworth's old leech-gatherer the available sticks in these larch-plantations seem to grow remoter & remoter! But the conclusion of all this rigmarole is that I *shan't* be coming to Rhos. But do keep in your dear skull (whether *Venedotian* or whatever Prof. Fleure w^d. say it was!) the fact that except between Monday Aug 13 and Saturday Aug 18 when *as per usual* I really literally go into *RELIGIOUS RETREAT* (not very far away either) I shall be & so will Phyllis be here in Number 7 longing to welcome you (if possible in company with our "Mutuals" the Morgans) if any possible chance gave you wings – God! I shall study your Aug 8th adjudication with interest *in print*. But alas! I'm hopeless at the language spoken. Tis my absolute lack as I tell you of any *ear for music* or musical inflexion.

O my dear Iorwerth, I cannot tell you how I commend your good vow *not* to reply to K. Rhys's attack. I never attack though I sometimes defend. God! tho' I used to be the very devil of a Debater on *the Platform*! But I'm no good at Debate with a pen for I am incurably pathologically analytical & *very long-winded* & romantic too to the obscurest rims of the horizons! And of course in controversy it's all *condensed*. You certainly "started something" as we say on the other side over that *Sovereignty business* & now De Valera is going ahead with it. But I confess frankly I share with the *Infernal Traveller* (tho' Vergil made him blush for it) a wicked old-wife's gloating joy in watching a mental battle over nice aesthetic or political or racial or religious points. In fact I have just written to K. Rhys whom I have a strong curiosity to set my Phorhyad eye on, by which I *don't* mean the *evil eye* but the analytical eye! telling him that it was decent of him to send me *Wales gratis*. My good friend Prof. Gwyn Jones our co-regionalist with "*Harri* of Monmouth" who was so sweet to me as my Aberystwyth host clearly feels that a fellow-novelist ought to order his little pleasures in the Magazine line & pay for them and no doubt he's right . . . At the same time 'tis very agreeable to receive a lively controversial Forum of furious civil wars sent to me without order or cash! I say when I wrote to him to thank him for this Number I strongly commented on crowding its pages with the hot dust of gladiatorial battles – though I can tell you I did not express anything beyond my pleasure in hoverings & waverings in these arenas of "dadl" as the luckless "timer" or whatever they call the chap does with Prize Fighters. But I did say to Phyllis: "I pray to God Iorwerth does *not* reply". For I know that this vow of yours is the wise course – though the other course – for you to get angry & hit back – would, if it weren't *you*, be mighty entertaining sport to a wicked half-Sais!

But what I long to do one day (only I didn't reveal this personal reaction to the daring editor) is to answer in a veritable torrent of my best Wild West oratory that article by *Wade-Evans* w[h]. made me see red! Do tell me when *next* you have a spare quarter of an hour *who* this gentleman is for I know naught of him except his name & what I associate with *that* I've forgotten!

But when as today there comes the current "Seren" y Bala & I read the death & burial of "John Jones of Llwyn Teg" in a noble classical simplicity with a touch worthy of the Greek anthology of the dust lying light on his bones I feel that you are O so right in making the *language* the thing! And I feel that it was *y Beibl* that did for Wales what the Catholic Church did for Ireland. "A'r iaith Gymraeg yw'r unig reswm tros barhad pob sefydliad cenedlaethol sydd yng Nghymru – yn syndod i gefnogwyr rhai ohonynt, ond dyna'r gwir".* I.P. *Y Llenor*, 1941.

Well! I must stop. But what I feel is that we Anglo-Welsh are *welcome to go to the limit* as long as we are *humble & reverent* towards those who can *speak & write the language*.

Yr old vacillator John the weather cock.

* 'And the Welsh language is the only reason for the continued existence of every national institution in Wales . . . much to the amazement of the supporters of some of them, but this is the truth.' – From Iorwerth C. Peate, 'Anthropoleg a Phroblemau Cyfoes' (= Anthropology and Modern Problems) in *Y Llenor*, 1941, pp. 17–24.

In the third paragraph of this letter, J.C.P. refers to 'K. Rhys's attack'. Mr Rhys was editor of a magazine entitled *Wales*, and in his 'Comments' in the Summer 1945 number he indulged in an attack upon my weekly literary feature in *Y Cymro* newspaper. The feature, which I edited under the pen-name *Y Gwerinwr*, was entitled *Cymru Heddiw* (= Wales Today). Mr Rhys chose to refer to me as a 'would-be literary Fuehrer . . . *Y Gwerinwr* in his *Cymru Heddiw* comic strips'. It was such a farrago of personal abuse that, naturally, I took no notice of it.

The 'sovereignty business' referred to an article which I published at the time pleading with the Nationalists to re-think their attitude towards national sovereignty and Dominion status in view of the peculiarly close geographical relationship of Wales with England.

Professor Gwyn Jones (see Letter 3) was the editor of an excellent monthly magazine, *The Welsh Review*, which unfortunately ceased publication with the Winter 1948 number. Incidentally, the last number included 'Amis and Amile', a translation into English of Mr Saunders Lewis's *Amlyn ac Amig*. This play is not represented in the recently-published volume *Presenting Saunders Lewis* (University of Wales Press, Cardiff, 1973).

The late Rev. A. W. Wade-Evans, a native of Pembrokeshire, spent his life as an Anglican cleric in Essex, etc. But he was a fervid Welsh nationalist. A man of erratic genius and scholarship, he published much on the Age of the Saints and the Dark Ages in Wales. In *Wales*, Summer 1945, he published an article on 'The Welsh Mind', an attack on a letter circulated in January 1943, signed by eighty graduates of the University of Wales supporting the candidature of Professor W. J. Gruffydd in the by-election of 1943 of an M.P. for the then University of Wales constituency, Gruffydd was elected. This was the article which aroused J.C.P.'s anger.

32

7 Cae Coed / Corwen / Merionethshire
Feb 14 1946 / St Valentine's Day!

My dear Iorwerth

How happy I am to get this considerate & affectionate little word from you and I can tell you I have read every sentence of this printed article with absorbed & fascinated interest. I find myself in sympathy and agreement with almost all you say here; and I am proud indeed to be quoted by you.

I think we are thinking along the same lines save that I have come to associate the word "love" – you know what I mean – with various aspects of Christianity that I can't help feeling the world could get on better without, by substituting kindness & common-sense. Again my own temperamental bias is in favour of shaking off the bad elements of Nationalism rather by feeling ourselves into the "mass-community" of the whole world, "my parish is the world" as you quote here, than of concentrating on these regional centres of fellowship and trying *within these differentiated little communities* to feel as if we belonged to a big family & are "members one of another". It is I think more in harmony with my secret and individual conscience and categorical imperative, and perhaps with something solitary in my nature, to try to be as you say & as St. Paul says tolerant to all other individuals while at the same time I am constantly imagining & telling myself stories about a real Utopian *U.N.O.* that includes the whole mass-community of the round earth. The reading or hearing on the air of Mr M. Murry makes me feel rebellious anti-social & anarchistic à la Bakunin! but there's a heap of truth in his words.

Yes! I think highly my dear Iorwerth of this improved letter-head of thine! it's an excellent-looking and a true one! Aye! what a spirited Being & talented our EVAN ROBERTS is – God! & what a lesson in putting up with physical handicaps! These curst ulcers of mine, my friend, are so slow in healing up. I stay in bed. I live on liquids. I write hardly any letters. But they *won't* heal up. – However! I am in excellent spirits and I've just had the *Galley Proofs* of my enormously huge book on Rabelais in which I emphasize the influence of Cymru-via-Llydaw upon his writing.

Well I'm too invalidish to say more now but *we'll talk again*!

Yr aff^{te}. admirer & friend
John C.P.

Knowing of his interest in such subjects, I had sent to J.C.P. a copy of my address to the students of Carmarthen Presbyterian College on 'Nonconformity and Culture' ('Anghydffurfiaeth a Diwylliant'; see my *Ym Mhob Pen* . . . (Gwasg Aberystwyth, 1948), pp. 57–67). His comments throw an interesting light on his personal philosophy. Though at the time J.C.P. did not know it, Middleton Murry was a personal friend whom I greatly admired. The greatest of his virtues was honesty; to this he added, as Mr Hugh I'Anson Fausset once pointed out, 'an inability to compromise'. T. S. Eliot and others have stressed his outstanding achievements as a literary critic. 'There can be few writers', wrote the late Sir Richard Rees, 'who have approached with such profound insight the crucial problems of our age and, in particular, few, if any, who have been so selflessly devoted to illuminating the genius of other men.'

In the last paragraph, 'Cymru-via-Llydaw' = Wales-via-Brittany.

33

7 Cae Coed / Corwen / Merionethshire
March 27 1947

My dear Iorwerth

I do indeed thank you for giving me this *fine* copy of your most arresting article on the Crwth the Pibgorn & the Harp. I've already read it twice over so as to get into my unmusical old skull the actual facts it contains as to at least the *shape* of the instruments. I had certainly no idea that there were bag-pipes too!

Well my dear friend my general health I'm thankful to be able to tell you is ever so much better. I have however quite lost the use of my right eye.

I am afraid our mutual ally at Llandderfel that gallant historian Mr Evan Roberts doesn't recover as quickly as I thought he would but I *have* had & not so long ago a nice characteristic letter from him.

I still find it wisest & safest to go on living a severely recluse sort of life but I go again my morning walks on the Berwyns – only missed one morning in all that frost & snow – and I am now beginning very slowly my final chapter of my long Romance of Corwen in A.D. 499 the last year of the 5th century – but as my book on Rabelais written 2 or 3 years ago is still unpublished – though the page-proof has for a year been corrected and a Librarian friend has made a *Preface* the *first time* that my unscholarly slap-dash Muse has ever aspired to a Preface – whether I'll live to see this Romance in the hands of my friends I cannot tell! I read each week with constant interest your critical articles in the *Cymro* and I find myself almost invariably in agreement with your view-point.

Yrs as heretofore

John.

The article referred to was 'Welsh Musical Instruments', *Man*, 1947, p. 17.

34

7 Cae Coed / Corwen / Merionethshire
April 17 1947

My dear Iorwerth

Sure! it'll be wonderful to get a glimpse of you if you *do* come thro' Corwen & we both – Phyllis & I – pray indeed that fate will arrange that you do come this way.

Yes I had a nice word from Evan Roberts this very morn & he refers to your lecture of May 9th & he also refers to past and future visits from 3 striking Personalities, more different from one another than are the persons of the Trinity!

1. The Catholic Archbishop Mac Grath (we'll put him first!).

2. Bob Owen of Croesor of whom I've heard very often: but have not the faintest notion of what he's really like.

3. Mr *T. E. Nicolas* who *has* been here & whose personality – tho' what person of any Trinity to call him I don't know! – & know pretty exactly where I am or am not "with" him.

I am very glad and so is Phyllis to hear about that Broadcasted Poem on the 29th April at 7.30. Yes I should say it is praise what W. J. Gruffydd said of it but I doubt if I get its quality *till I see it in print*. I am hopelessly under the Shakespearean *Curse* of the man "who has *no music in himself* nor is not moved by concord of sweet sounds" that I have to *see* the words of a poem before I do them justice. You know Iorwerth I really believe there is some kind of *poetic aura projected by the look of the words* of both fine poetry and fine prose that evokes a response – at least in my absolutely unmusical nature – but a nature *very* responsive to *landscape painting* rather than of any musical sound.

So long! this till we see you on your way in May. God! yes I bet you *are* nigh overpowered by this *Folk Museum*. Well!

Well!, as you hint, I fancy you're not the first to find a Dream come True to be one devil of a business to cope with.

Yrs as always
John.

I pray I shan't forget in the excitement of seeing you all the questions I want to ask you.

The late Dr Michael MacGrath was then Roman Catholic Archbishop of Cardiff; an Irishman, a fine Welsh speaker, and above all a true Christian; he was a good friend of Mr. Evan Roberts. Robert Owen (O.B.E., Hon.M.A.) of Croesor, Merioneth, was at first a quarryman who came to be known throughout Wales as Bob Owen. A bibliophile, he collected an incredible number of Welsh books, pamphlets and manuscripts, particularly of Welsh-American and Welsh-Australian interest. Thomas Evan Nicholas, a Pembrokeshire man, at one time a Congregational minister, settled in Aberystwyth as a dentist. He was a lifelong Socialist who wrongfully suffered prison during the Second World War. He published several volumes of poetry, notably a volume of sonnets composed in Swansea and Brixton prisons. Detained in Swansea prison under the notorious 18b regulation, he was not allowed writing-paper, and wrote a long poem for competition at the National Eisteddfod, on prison toilet-paper!

The broadcast poem to which J.C.P. referred was a sonnet-sequence entitled *Cymru* (= Wales) – see *Canu Chwarter Canrif* (Denbigh, 1957), pp. 52–3.

The national Welsh Folk Museum was established at St. Fagans, near Cardiff, in 1947.

35

7 Cae Coed / CORWEN / Merionethshire

June 9 1947

My dear Iorwerth

Thrilled indeed I can tell you was I when I opened yesterday Sunday the 8th last week's number of "*Y Cymro*" & there was confronted – turning the pages hurriedly over, as I always do, resisting, like Christian or Faithful passing thro' the streets of Vanity Fair, the alluring pictures & provocative topical topics on the way and falling upon the Heddiw Gwerin page, yes! was confronted then by *the magic letters in Big Type* "DOSTOIEVSKY". Aye! but I was so proud & jubilant; & had indeed *"the Swelled Head"*, as we say in the States, for at least the next twelve hours! For it is such a Splendid Review – aye! it sure is! & it "gets the number" of your aged friend *and* his great master to a tune to a nicety to a hair rarely, almost *never*, reached in a review in *any* paper!

It *was* such a delight to both Phyllis & me to get that happy glimpse of you with Mr John Morgan that day but I never thought I'd cast such a crust of a loaf upon such Waters of LIFE when I saved you one of those little yellow books.

Yrs as ever,

John.

The 'little yellow book' was, of course, J.C.P.'s *Dostoievsky* (John Lane, The Bodley Head, London, 1946) which he had inscribed with an appropriate medieval-Welsh quatrain.

36

Corwen, Merionethshire
November the 10th 1947

My dear Iorweth

I do thank you indeed from my heart for this book, for now I have got those 5 grand sonnets you gave me in type to enjoy in print. I have already become pretty familiar with them for I have kept them from

> Goleuaist ti holl erwau fy mhlentyndod

down to

> Dy holl anwyldeb di hyd ddiwedd byd.

With your poetry for of course you are a real poet Iorwerth my danger is to miss lots of the subtlties I wouldn't be missing in English and *in spite of this* to be so proud of myself that I can get real strong poetical pleasure from this poetry in the tongue of my father's fathers as to be tempted to fuse something of the pleasure of this pride with the too simple and not subtle enough pleasure derived from what among the easier and more obvious effects of the poetry, its thoughts, its moods, its images, its imagination, as these can be enjoyed with the imponderable overtones & undertones such as we have the power to catch in our own mother-tongue but to catch which in any other tongue demands a scholarship – and more than that perhaps; a philological *genius* you might say – totally beyond my mental or aesthetic power; and by this same fusion of the pleasure of pride that I can enjoy your poetry in this same simple and un-subtle way with the actual, direct, real, though necessarily restricted pleasure that I get from your poetry as an objective thing in itself quite apart from my "glorying" as St Paul w^d. say in being able to get any pleasure at all – being so little of a linguist – in the poetry of the tongue of my ancestors as it is used by a real poet. I won't my dear Iorwerth read this convoluted sentence over for fear I'd find I'd not only failed to express what I wanted to, but even failed to keep the laws of syntax and grammar in my attempt to do so!

But you know I feel *just the same* – being a born student but *not* alas! a born scholar – over the poetry of Villon, Verlaine, Horace, Vergil. I took a Horace (with a crib) with me to the Wrexham hospital when I was ill and got a lot of pleasure from much of it but trying to analyze this pleasure I believe I found or find perhaps I ought to say – three distinct elements –

1. The pride of being able to get such pleasure at all! a sort of aesthetic snobbishness!

2. The direct pleasure of the poetic images etc etc.

3. The special and quite peculiar beauty of Latin *as Latin.*

This rambling thanks, Iorwerth old friend, needs no acknowledgement or reply – in fact I hereby command and implore you *not* to reply for *no news* between you & me who understand each other so well *means good news.*

Yrs as ever

John.

I had sent J.C.P. (Letter 34) a sonnet-sequence which now appeared in my book, *Y Deyrnas Goll a Cherddi Eraill* (= The Lost Kingdom and other poems) (Caerdydd, 1947). The long 'convoluted' sentence in J.C.P.'s first paragraph is an excellent example of what he described as his 'serpentine manner' of writing.

37

Sunday night / Nov 16 / 1947 / 7 Cae Coed / Corwen

My dear Iorwerth

Just a line to tell you only 2 things! But this scrawl needs no reply, old friend, for you are a very busy man while I am an ancient Pensioner at liesure [sic] so it'll only distress me if you reply to this telepathic vibration across the hills between us. For you and I (as I know from reading your excellent comment on this new theological book in this recent *Cymro*) understand each other curiously well without need of writing! Aye! How well I follow this word about the *"undeb"* [= union] in the *cemetery* compared with the divergences *that are alive*!

The 1st. thing is that "*Y Deyrnas Goll*" grows on me more & more. I've read no poetry in this tongue I like better or can follow more easily.

The 2^{d}. thing is – in case your path is crossed or your desk is burdened by this little collection of *old* essays of mine *re-published* by the Druid Press of Carmarthen I don't want you to blame this Press – or its characteristic Editor & Publisher (whom you have met but I have never seen) – for what is really & truly *three quarters my fault* & one quarter the fault of the exigencies of *all* publishers at this epoch but it was like this. This collection of old essays – well! essays writ in these last 13 years – since Phyllis & I and her mother & aunt settled down in this excellent couple of next-door little new houses! – was to appear *quite a long while ago* last Xmas I fancy it was – but when I thought the publication was immanent [sic] & there was no time for delay I was seized with a desire to write hurriedly quickly and so to say *at one break* a complete *new & fresh* essay! I am as I've often told you I expect a lecturer, a story-teller, preacher, & speaker (even an orator!) *first* & *a writer secondly* & therefore *not being an artist* I don't worry over punctuation or even syntax and *take little or take no interest in any writings of mine once they've been printed*! So to make this little book — for w^{h}. as with most of my books I let the publisher invent the title* & I *rather* like this odd one tho' maybe it

---

* The title was obviously suggested by his own description of himself (*Autobiography*, p. 26) as 'obstinately Cymric'.

should have been *Cymro* but maybe not – I am not sure & do not greatly care either! to make, I say, *interesting to myself* I implored K[eidrych] R[hys] whom I have never met to let me add an up-to-date essay & also, so as to *save the time* of sending it to my old typist in Dorchester who alone *can read my hand at sight*, to let me send this new essay in *long hand MSS*. This accounts therefore for the typographical errors in this same *printed* final essay entitled "*My Philosophy*" and it also accounts for the fact that my usual *rush of platform awen* so overwhelming as speech but so upsetting to all good craftsmanship *in style* is even more in evidence than usual!

[no signature]

The book referred to is *Obstinate Cymric: Essays* 1935–47 (The Druid Press Ltd., Carmarthen, 1947).

Awen (in the final sentence) has no exact equivalent in English; the University of Wales Dictionary gives 'poetic gift, genius or inspiration, the muse'.

38

Corwen

Nov 19th 1947

Only a scrawl f'annwyl gyfaill to tell you I'l let Redwood A. have your good words. Alas! he is now suffering one of his periodic attacks of a half physical half mental kind a sort of nervous breakdown but at once less or more serious, but I've just had a line from him himself to say he is better for wh. I am deeply thankful. Yes I see him normally *every Saturday* he comes up from The Square where he lodges with lovely people – the best in Corwen, after (of course) our Mutual Friends – and reads his newest and oldest writings aloud to me. He reads his own poetry *beautifully* a rare thing with poets. I am in wholehearted agreement, as a mere learner, with all this wondrously satisfactory passage from Prof W.J.G. I *do* congratulate you & shall be, I can see, steadily doing so more & more as I go on with your work. No it's this curst queer illness of his that has delayed his acknowledging *Y Deyrnas Goll*. But he *is* better and in a few weeks we'll be sitting together here studying your book.

Alas! my friend I would to God I could tell you when my Rabelais *will* appear! I have to force myself to be a philosopher about this and as stoical as Pantagruel himself! But it *will* come out. It will, it *will*! They've got it all ready for binding in corrected Book-Proof & with o such a careful Index done for love by Mr. G. Turner boss of the Public Library of Richmond, Surrey! It's the first Index I've ever had! But this "Obstinate Cymric" I see has one!!

Well Good Luck and I am thrilled to hear of your Review in Good Time & Due Time in *Y Cymro*. We were so pleased at your "atoch eich dau".

Yrs ever my friend

John.

J. Redwood Anderson used to send me copies of his books as they appeared, and I responded with such volumes as *Y Deyrnas Goll*. The reference to Professor Gruffydd was to an appreciation by him of the same volume.

The reference in the final paragraph was to my forthcoming review of *Obstinate Cymric* in *Y Cymro*.

Atoch eich dau refers to my greetings 'to you both'.

39

Corwen

Monday Dec 15 1947

My dear Friend

I was deeply touched by your subtle penetrating & absolutely true "adolygiad" of my little volume "Cymro Ystyfnig" in "the Cymro". That last sentence of yours with its lovely & tender irony worthy of *Renan* himself – aye! but I adored it! In fact I have a feeling that there's a peculiar & quite special atmosphere or aroma about your pen that in that castle of yours in its queer mingling of austere *Intellectual Positivism* & the Method and Secret of Jesus makes me think so strongly of Renan or at least of the *impression* left on my memory by what I've read *long ago* of his! I think your present position in Welsh Literature is *unique* and I think this column of yours in "Y Cymro" is very *very* important & the spear-head of a *New Cymru*. I've been reading with fascinated interest every word of them. How on earth you have managed to write this thin vol of such really *noble poetry* in the midst of all your Museum activities the Lord only knows! You know you really *are* a wonder, Iorwerth; & I cannot be *too proud* of such a world of understanding as this article contains.

This scrawl of thanks is *not to be acknowledged* for your time is too well spent & your labours too heavy as it is!

Ever yr grateful old friend

John.

This letter refers to my review (*Y Cymro*, December 12, 1947) of *Y Cymro Ystyfnig* (= *Obstinate Cymric*).

40

Corwen

Dec 23 1947

Yes my dear friend that *was* truly a *strikingly unfair unjust* and profoundly *prejudiced* attack on your poetry! It was an attack inspired by a dislike of the very essence of your nature! How you poets do by publishing your feelings tie yourselves like so many Saint Sebastians to *stakes* for those *astrologically hostile* to your essential being to shoot arrows at – & the nearer these arrows get to sensitive or vital spots the more there ariseth in these alien hearts exultant joy!

You see in your other works & *even in your ideas* you can have your enemies and you can hit back & give as good as you take; but it's his soul that a poet lays bare! *He can't help it* – And that gives the enemies of the lord their chance! I can see the same thing happening with my neighbour R[edwood] A[nderson] whom you *did* help so & so magnanimously championed, Iorwerth. It *did* please me so.

Your old John.

I cannot recall the 'attack' mentioned here or its author.

41

7 Cae Coed / Corwen / Merionethshire / N. Wales
July 8 1948

My dear I. C. P.

I've only just realized how alike our *Initials* are! So this is I.C.P. to I.C.P. for 'tis hard to *tell apart a capital* "i" *and* "j"!!

Well I do thank you for this Perfect Collection of *Penetrations into literature and reality* – God! my friend, you really do stand like Aaron between the Dead-Living *Saeson* & the Living-dead *Cymry* waking them both up! You are far the most important & most valuable & indispensable Pillar of the Principality today – the Subtle Double-Languaged Principality, the Nation of – what's that queer-looking & rather scaring word these psychiatrists use? Zizophrenes or something like that! Because *you alone* (& I tell you I *study carefully & analytically* every word each Sunday of the Faner the Cymro and the Seren) really follow the topical intelligentsia discussions in the New Statesman the Time & Tide the Spectator etc etc & it w^d. *almost* seem the American radical papers too! – *not* to *whet your own rapier* or *grind your own axe* as other well-known Critics *in Cymraeg* do – but to honestly *instruct* & *inform* your Welsh readers as to what *is being thought on all sides* over the border and over the Channel & over the Atlantic! You are my dear Iorwerth the *only honest teacher* of the *only true university of Wales* that is to say the *invisible* Sunday School of its authentic Nonconformity!

. . . . . .

Yrs as ever John.

I had sent J.C.P. a copy of my book *Ym Mhob Pen* . . ., a collection of critical essays. His reaction was typical but misleading, for I did not merit his superlatives.

42

7 Cae Coed / Corwen / Merionethshire / N. Wales
March 9th 1949

My dear Iorwerth

Forgive my long silence but I've treated my brothers & sisters in the same way (though I've struggled to write *pretty* regularly to our old Llandderfel historian for it's really amazing his spirit and courage with all the weakness & pain he has to contend with) with the excuse *partly* justifiable – but of course none of our natural human excuses are ever – as you theologians are the ones to know best! – absolutely so! of my one *Cyclopean eye*!

But you'll be sympathetic I know, my dear Iorwerth, with my bolder & better excuse for being a bad correspondent. I never know with these damned words in "ant" & "ent" whether it's an "a" or an "e"; so I generally as in lots of *other cases* put a scriggle & let my poor old typist-friend (Mrs Meech of the "Typing Bureau" 24 High West Street Dorchester Dorset) worry! She's typed for me since 1929 without a pause & can read my worst convolutions & alterations serpentine twists & turns! And tho' I'm better than she at *Mythology* – she's better than I am at spelling.

Well now Iorwerth my friend to my grand excuse being so wretched a *correspondint -dunt -dant* namely the final chapters of my long Romance about *Corwen* in *A.D.* 499 entitled "Porius" after that stone in the foothills of the mountains above Bala "In hoc tumulo hic jacet Porius Christianus fuit". I hope the ghost of the real Porius won't bring me bad luck for the one I've buried under that stone (tho' a Christian) *was a Roman* . . . & only grand-father to my real hero another Porius, i.e. Porius ab Einion ab Iddawc ab Edeyrn *ab Cunedda*! a 5th cousin, I pretend, of Gildas's "Maelgwn" or "Malcunus" of Deganwy! I took my final page, i.e. (another "i.e." or idiot's entrance!) page 2811 in my long sprawl up to the Gaer here & snugly ensconced against the north-east wind = that deepest *stone-craters* in the wall or stone-chambers & waited for some sort of Inspiration *in situ* for my last paragraph & I really *did* get it! . . . but I make no conjecture as to whence it came! But to a daring romance – I daresay more daring than historical; for I introduce both *Arthur* & *Merlin* bringing them *both* on a campaign against the Saeson *to Edeyrnion*!

But aye, my dear Iorwerth, I expect you can guess & believe how long I'll take correcting the type of this huge volume & whether it'll appear in print while I am still walking as a man & not as a ghost I do not know! Well, I must stop. I do hope you are in good heart & good spirits. The Cymro isn't the same at all without those articles . . . not the same at all.

Yr faithful & affe^{te}. friend

J. C. Powys.

After editing and frequently writing the '*Cymru Heddiw*' column in *Y Cymro* for six years, I had given up the work in 1948, when the development of the new Welsh Folk Museum, which opened in July of that year, demanded my attention during leisure- as well as official office-hours. Living now in a flat in St. Fagans Castle, I was constantly available. To J.C.P. the disappearance of *Y Gwerinwr* from his weekly newspaper was a blow, as the last sentence in Letter 42 indicates; he mentions it again in Letter 43. To some extent it diminished the tie between us, and not surprisingly he blamed (Letter 43) the paper itself for allowing me to go.

The Porius stone had stood on what was then War Office property at Trawsfynydd, Merioneth; to ensure its safety from being destroyed by gun-fire, etc., it was removed to the National Museum of Wales to take its place in the collection of pre-Norman stone monuments there exhibited. A replica was set up on its traditional site. J.C.P. had strong views about the Porius inscription (see Letters 43 and 45, and notes). His description of himself waiting 'for some sort of Inspiration' to finish his long Corwen romance is interesting, although the reference to the 'deepest stone-craters' and 'stone-chambers' is somewhat incoherent.

43

7 Cae Coed / Corwen / Merionethshire
March 14 1949

My dear Iorwerth

I am so sorry about that awful business of your Mother's death & your having no more any personal link with Llanbryn Mair; & having to go there & fix up all & leave all is the devil. The death of a mother & the razing out of these old associations & having to do it all yourself is an experience that makes anyone feel old & I do fully agree that as you get older you grow more & more sympathetic to your parents & (apart from sympathy *or* revolt) you grow a lot more *interested* in them! But to lose a mother makes anyone realize the loneliness of the human self as nothing else does though of course the actual *sense of loss* is stronger for our *mate* whether man or woman . . . but may *that* hour – for both you & me & for *our* mates – *be far off* my dear friend!

O no! I had not the least idea that the *Maen Porius* left at Trawsfynydd was only a *copy*!! I've just looked the point up in Rhys' Lectures on *Welsh Philology* 1877 (when I was 5 years old!) & he quotes just as you do here this XPL or KPI but he takes for granted it's 'Christianus'. But that *"Planus Homo"* business certainly makes no difference to my story my title or my own belief. I simply cannot believe for one moment that in those old days anybody would call themselves or – still less – much less! be called so by their relatives or admirers or setters up of stones. I think I have never heard of such foolish unpsychological, *un-common-sense fantastical palaeontology* or philology or whatever the word is in my life as to turn the "Khi" into a *Homo Planus*, "a plain man"! It's absurd! It's *comical*! My old friend Louis Marlow née [*sic*] Wilkinson will laugh at me over this for he always ridicules my really not unfashionable chat about the "common man" in my various *tracts for the times* . . . *He* says 'tis "uncommon common men"! Well! we need, you & I are I know agreed on this, we need lots of un-common *common men*! Well *you* were too un-common for that Gwerinwr column – *that*'s clear enough!

Yr affec^t. & faithful John.

The word in the Porius inscription which J.C.P. reads as 'Christianus' (following Sir John Rhŷs in his *Lectures on Welsh Philology*, p. 390) appears on the stone as P✧ANUS. J.C.P. takes the P and sloping L to represent the normal abbreviation of *Christ-*. But in 1885 (*Arch. Camb.*, p. 145) D. R. Thomas read the word as *planus*, and in *Arch. Camb.*, 1897, pp. 197–8, Rhŷs accepted the new reading, and returned to a discussion of it in *Y Cymmrodor*, 1905, where he suggested that *planus* meant 'low, humble, simple'. Some students, however, were attracted to the meaning derived from the Hellenistic use of the word, 'a wanderer'. J.C.P., however, would have none of this (see Letter 45). The late Egerton Phillimore, with his genius for settling philological problems, in an article on ' "*Homo planus*" and Leprosy in Wales' (*Arch. Camb.*, 1920, pp. 224–50), translated *homo planus* here as 'flat-faced man', comparing the adjective with *wynepclawr* in Welsh and *cláreinech* in Irish.*

* I acknowledge with gratitude the valuable help given by Professor Idris Ll. Foster, Jesus College, Oxford, and Dr H. N. Savory, Keeper of Archaeology in the National Museum of Wales, Cardiff, in the preparation of this note.

44

7 Cae Coed / Corwen / Merioneth / N. Wales

Sept 13 1949

My dear Iorwerth

What a pleasure was your good letter to Phyllis & me. Till this Thursday the 15th we've got my 2 youngest sisters *Katie & Lucy* otherwise Miss Philippa Powys and Mrs Penny. My eldest sister *Gertrude* the *Painter* is off this autumn to visit our youngest brother W. E. P. in Kenya; this I can tell you is a bit of an agitation to us all for she is 70 & a very bad traveller! But all the same a gallant woman for she has already despatched by ship all her painting apparatus! That country is something to paint but not free from dangers for my brother had his *hand* nearly amputated by a lion lately & his "jeep" a thing I've *never seen* to my knowledge, in peril from a Rhinocerus!

O I do so agree with you about Llewelyn's Cradle of God. It's one of my favourite books of his & I've read that volume lately and I thought the close of it was *just as you say*. I am rejoiced about your being Pres. of the Univ. Philosophical Section. They chose well & the "Welsh Nonconformist Mind" is a *perfect subject* for your address in a year's time. O no I don't think *Professional Philosophers* i.e. *sef* – *Metaphysicians* with *Systems* are *a patch upon* the great soothsayers like Heraclitus & Pythagoras & Goethe & Rabelais and Nietzsche & my own modern favourite philosopher *William James*!

Heaven! But you *sure have* had some visitors this last year! Well, old friend, Phyllis & I hope for better luck another time you are round this way. She has seen Mrs Morgan and heard such good tales of her & Catrin's trip abroad. Please give my homage to your wife though I've never yet met her. Phyllis & my sisters have gone by train officially to Blaenau Ffestiniog today but from their lateness I fancy they've gone *further* perhaps even to *Harlech*!

Yrs as ever

John.

P.S. [on envelope] You must promise to let me see some copy of that address when *next Sept* 1950 comes round. For you are the only one in Wales who really (of this I am absolutely certain) upholds the deep *dirgelwch* of that yes of that Evangelical Mystery of early Xtianity which William Blake as well as Rabelais divined. It has become a sort of *stunt* to make sport & *cheap sport* of these things amongst these accurst *ffug-Gymry*!

Dirgelwch = Mystery. *Ffug-Gymry* = Sham-Welshmen.

45

7 Cae Coed / Corwen / Merioneth / N. Wales
Saturday Aug 18 1951

F'annwyl Gyfaill

I do thank you ever so for this excellent clear & official & final & definitive (if I spell that technical printing and publishing word correctly) article on the *Gorsedd* & *Eisteddfod*. I have always been confused over this matter & *never till now* had a clear notion of the truth about it but I accept (as they say) *as gospel* every word in this paper of yours & I am very thankful to have it. Phyllis & I can remember when we first met you some fifteen or sixteen years ago – think of that! – when the Morgans brought you to call and you then threw doubt on the Gorsedd of Iolo Morganwg and Mr Morgan said "if Iolo's Gorsedd is all fabrication it's up to you young men (I don't suppose he actually said "up to" I must be Americanizing his remark a bit!) to set the Gorsedd *and* Eisteddfod on a sound basis".

It's unfortunate for me that you and Professor Gruffydd both take that odd-looking P L *mixture of letters* to mean *Planus* because I followed Sir John Rhys (for of course personally I am totally in the dark over these archaeological nuances and unfortunately at the moment I can't quote to you the passage from Rhys w^h. is in one of his volumes of lectures & *in the index too* where he goes carefully through all the *stone inscriptions* in the *different Counties of Wales* & this one was in the *Notes about Merioneth* – but no doubt you know the volume – I cannot unluckily quote it or even I am sorry to say recall its title but it is full of Ogam inscriptions if I am not making it up! I gave or lent I forget which this book of Sir John Rhys to my Publisher to make sure *he* realized anyway that I had *some* proper & accepted authority behind me in my interpretation of this ticklish syllable on this Porius Stone! But I little thought Sir John was leading me wrong! I had followed him so loyally ever since in my twenties I gave my *trial university extension lecture* at the Oxford Summer School, which I based on Rhys's book on the Arthurian Legend – a book I have often read & re-read since those early days but as it was published in *1890* I daresay it's a bit old-fashioned in its interpretation! But I never thought Rhys w^d. lead me *quite* as astray as this! Do tell me – but I *must* wait till you return from Sweden before I bother you with such technicalities! – whether you think *any* modern Welsh scholar *still agrees with Rhys* over this particular *Porius Stone*? I *do* now seem to recall – damn it! I wish I had that book under my hand! – a funny looking mixture of letters rather like a P with a cross across it some way and "ianus" after it! Anyway as I've seen so many queer abbreviations of "*Christus*" I took it & swallowed it without a further thought and I was staggered when someone told me that there even *existed* a *totally different interpretation*! I've just been looking up this word in my classical dictionary and I *do* see the Professor's *Ciceronian quotation* for *charlatan tramp impostor* – I feel as if it were my own grave rather than Porius's! for I am used to being called (as most University *Extension* lecturers are!) mountebank and *improbus rogue*! But, *seriously*, f'annwyl gyfaill Iorwerth, *does* it seem possible to you as a matter of ordinary secular un-scholarly *lay* common sense that a *stone w^d. be put up solemnly in those days* to a poor common rover or wanderer or juggler or tramp? still less to a rascal or vagabond and charlatan? Do you know of *any other such* memorial? Is it not *more likely* that this curious *jumble of letters* – P↲ – should represent some *monograph of Christ* oddly and *queerly shortened* as it sometimes is, isn't it? I certainly do find however in my small *Homeric* Dictionary not to mention Liddell & Scott the Greek word πλαναω meaning *to make to rove*!! *to lead astray*!! and πλανός an impostor or one subject to fits!!

Well! I must not ramble on any more of my name sake Sir John! When you return from Sweden I'll send you a copy of Porius for you own private shelf and then you'll be in a better & more fully "briefed" position to see whether *your* John has been led astray by Sir John or not!

Anyway yrs as ever

John.

The 'paper' referred to in the first paragraph was my 'The Gorsedd of the Bards of Britain' in *Antiquity*, 1951, pp. 13–15.

For the Porius problem, see note on Letter 43.

46

7 Cae Coed / Corwen / Merioneth / N. Wales
Oct 29 1951

My dear Doctor

I do feel so ashamed of myself not to have thanked you before for this splendid Extrait de "Laos" Upsala. Your mention of *Mr Hartland* reminds me so vividly of my lectures for Univ. Extension (I forget for what University I was (just then) the Extender of *Exciting Topics* if not of anything more intense) in the old city of *Gloucester* where on one of my visits I stayed with Hartland but I regret to say that he a middle-aged gent & a very very *very* young student of *any* poetical subjects had quite a row over I've forgotten what – but I recall (as people do you know!) his parting shot at me – "You call yourself a lecturer – I would remind you that that word means to *read*. You ought to *write* your discourses *and read them*!" . . . I *now* like to think that this was because I was *not* a reader but a "rhetor" & had carried the vulgar herd away by my "rhetoric" in an opposite direction from that taken in his *writings* anyway by Mr Hartland! But, f'annwyl Gyfaill, teaching, neither by treatise nor by rhetoric, but by *pictures* is what you do here & I enjoy learning from you which is the best learning of all!

As always J. C. Powys

– in spite of our different views upon P L & also on the value of the writings of Master Timothy Lewis!

On returning from Sweden I had sent J.C.P. a copy of my paper on 'The Welsh Folk Museum and its Development' which had appeared in *Laos*, 1, pp. 169–79 (Stockholm, 1951). It was profusely illustrated, and I knew how J.C.P. liked to 'learn from pictures'.

Sidney Hartland of Gloucester was the well-known folk-lorist.

47

7 Cae Coed / Corwen / Merioneth / N. Wales
Nov 30th 1953

My dear Friend

I do indeed value your most kind thought in writing to me so sympathetically about Theodore's death. I am so very pleased with your words about my sister's book on Lace. It is so strange to me to think that now after Littleton & me who've been together all through our long life tho' now he's terribly crippled by arthritis at Glastonbury where he lives it is our sister Marian who is the next in age & I can so well recall her as a child of 2 or 3 in our field near one of those chestnut Avenues in Dorchester!

Well – good luck –

Yrs J. C. Powys.

48

7 Cae Coed / Corwen / Merionethshire
Thursday November 18th 1954

My dear Friend

I do thank you heartily – yes i'faith most heartily – for your very generous & friendly congratulations about the really good start of my "Atlantis". But for heaven's sake, my dear friend, *don't* go *an inch further* in your magnanimous effort over any Litt.D. honour for me: for the plain & simple reason that I'd have to refuse anything of the sort. And I'll tell you why – just exactly & truthfully why.

Old age though it hasn't interfered with my mania for writing stories and hasn't brought *arthritis* with it, as with my brother Littleton who was 80 last April, has intensified my dread of any sort of publicity to a nervous terror that has become almost an obsession. For over a year I haven't even gone down into the town – no! not even to see my old admired friend John Morgan himself! Yes this is the real secret reason of our move to Blaenau *the most difficult place to reach* within 50 miles! Once there I shall become an *absolute Hermit* (with the aid of my American friend Miss Playter who is still an American citizen). No my dear friend don't 'ee for a second think I don't appreciate your gesture on my behalf with the University, for I *most* sincerely *do*. It's just simply that I've become "funny", in plain words not a little *neurotic* about any public honour or university honour – coming from *any* direction – gives me something like pure terror or panic!

Here is our address – but we *shall not be there* I feel pretty certain – you know *how slowly* these things occur – *till* 1955 – 1 Waterloo, Bethania Blaenau Ffestiniog, Merionethshire.

No, I myself *don't* know the work of David Jones but my Miss Playter tells me she has heard his plays on the wireless.

With the best, as you know, from us both

yrs J. C. Powys.

Several attempts were made during the 1950s to persuade the University of Wales authorities to confer upon J.C.P. the degree of D.Litt. *honoris causa*. Several of his friends were active in this matter and he must have heard of it. In 1962 – many years too late – the University decided to confer upon him the degree of *Doctor in Litteris*. He died in 1963.

This letter, the last which I was to receive from him from Corwen, showed, like most of his letters from about 1950, signs of his advancing age and his determination to 'become an absolute Hermit'.

Seven hundred and fifty copies of this book
have been published of which this copy is number

139